eek-style lamb and salad CROQUE MONSIEUR Mussels
and strawberry parfait Many meals from one Ratatoui
ck IDEAS FOR... SPEEDY SNACKS Cheesy tuna mor
sage and lemon Chilled leek soup Step-by-step Fish bak
noodle Colcannon Baked brioche with peach
BANANA BREAD Quick ideas for...baked jacket potatoes
h red wine gravy Rice pudding CHICKEN CACCIATOR
osciutto, pear and parmesan salad Oven-baked mushro
noodles Minted asparagus and pea soup Fresh tuna
lemon cream PANZANELLA SALAD WITH CHICKEN
salad Macerated strawberries Vegetarian chilli be
ette Quesadillas Creamy pumpkin penne Pasta with
Y STEP-BY-STEP Gado gado Step-by-step
HOTPOT French toast POTATO, EGG AND BACON SAL
Chicken and mushroom pot pie Lemon and saf

salad   Mini bread and butter pudding   Eggs florenti

Chicken noodle soup   TUNA STEAK WITH SALSA ROS

ideas with... lamb cutlets   Spiced fruit and nut bread

POACHED PEARS   STEP-BY-STEP   Ricotta pancakes with fre

roasted quail with couscous   CARAMELISED BANANA

Quick ideas for... one-pot pasta meals   Refrigerator biscu

Berry whip   LEMON AND SAFFRON RISOTTO   STEP-BY-

Couscous and chickpea salad   Macaroni ba

Portuguese prawns   Step-by-step   Macerated strawberrie

mbed chicken fillets   Hearty potato soup   Brown fried

Prosciutto, pear and parmesan salad   Pasta primaver

MANY MEALS FROM ONE   BOLOGNESE SAUCE   Duck sa

Quick ideas for... stewed fruit   Fresh tuna and green bean

BEAN TORTILLA BASKET   Spiced spatchcock   step-by-

Prosciutto-stuffed chicken

COOKING FOR one *or* two

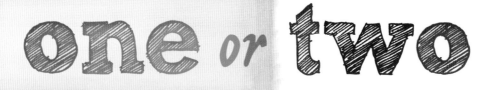

COOKING FOR
one *or* two

More than 100 recipes just for you... or maybe two

Reader's Digest

Contents

Treat yourself. In *Cooking for One or Two* we've created a wealth of easy-to-make, imaginative recipes specially for you.

If you are used to cooking for a crowd — or perhaps you don't usually cook at all — you might be surprised how simple it really is to make a meal for one or two people.

Think of all the advantages! There is much less fuss and bother. Weekly grocery shopping is simpler and far less time consuming, and complicated food preparation is minimised, leaving you in a more relaxed frame of mind to actually enjoy your meals. There are fewer fussy palates to please, too, so you can indulge your own tastebuds. And you won't be left with endless leftovers and mountains of washing up to deal with, as usually happens when cooking larger-scale recipes.

This book makes it so simple to cook solo, or in tandem. Each recipe has two separate ingredients lists — so you can choose whether to cook for one or to cook for two, without needing to do any maths when it comes to shopping, measuring and chopping.

We've brought together a range of meal ideas, from everyday to a little more special. We know there are times when it's hard to muster much enthusiasm to cook — which is why so many of the recipes are quick meals, one-pot and even no-cook dishes, all conveniently tagged so you can spot them at a glance. (You'll also see these recipes listed in our easy reference index on page 254.)

You'll even find clever downsized versions of comforting family favourites. Rather than bake a whole roast chicken, for example, try our fabulous Roast baby chicken on page 126. Our special 'Many Meals From One' features reveal how fantastically easy it is to turn one simple base recipe into many wonderful new dishes.

As well as helpful step-by-step recipes, you'll find plenty of tips for adapting dishes, and lots of special spreads featuring 'Quick Ideas' for snappy snacks and meals. You may find that resorting to those expensive takeaways or frozen TV dinners becomes a thing of the past. Try our heart-warming recipes and you'll soon be amazed what a lovely and very special pleasure it can be to cook just for one, or just for two.

You'll want to give this book to many people in your life – your mother, who may be on her own now, a close friend who may work punishingly long hours, or a favourite nephew who is starting out. Oh, and to yourself, of course!

The editors

Pared-down cooking for easy meals

Most of us will, at some point, find ourselves in a household of just one or two. Whether you are busy single person, an 'empty nester' or live in a household of two, rest assured it really doesn't take much effort to nourish yourself with delicious fuss-free meals.

Recipes just right for you

When living in a smaller household, many of us find ourselves thinking we're too busy to cook, or that it simply isn't worth cooking a meal for just one or two. We often then fall into the trap of resorting to soup-in-a-cup or cheese on toast every night. Our recipes prove, however, that it really is possible to enjoy great-tasting, imaginative meals without hours of preparation and cooking. Cooking for yourself, or just for two, doesn't mean missing out on hearty family-style favourites either. This book brings you all those recipes you love, reworked for one or two.

How this book works

We know you don't want to spend ages cooking and cleaning up, so our recipes keep the number of ingredients, preparation and kitchen utensils and equipment to a minimum. Where possible, we also use small jars and containers of basic ingredients to minimise wastage, and also give ideas for using up any leftovers.

Understandably, there'll be times when you don't have much time or inclination to cook — so to make it easier for you we've tagged recipes that are 'Quick' (on the table within 30 minutes), 'One-pot' and even 'No cook'.

Each recipe also has extra tips, such as serving suggestions, ideas for substituting ingredients or varying the recipe. And there are step-by-step photographs to help you achieve perfect results.

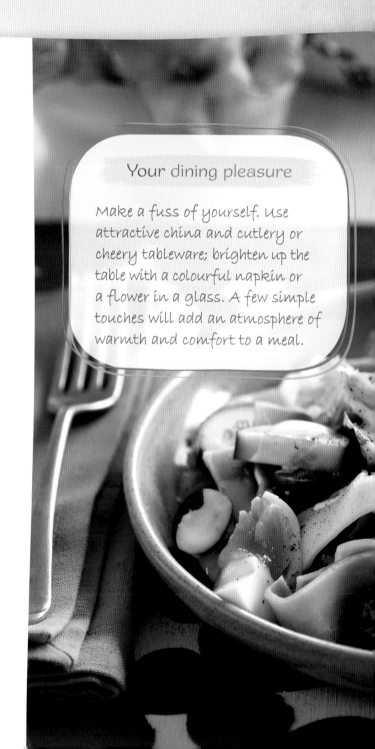

Your dining pleasure

Make a fuss of yourself. Use attractive china and cutlery or cheery tableware; brighten up the table with a colourful napkin or a flower in a glass. A few simple touches will add an atmosphere of warmth and comfort to a meal.

Cook for 1 or 2 – it's so easy

Recipes in this book feature dual ingredients lists, so you can see at a glance what you need for making one serve or two. This saves you having to do calculations as you shop and cook.

You will notice, however, that some recipes only have quantities 'For 2'. This is because for these recipes, it is more practical and efficient to make two serves, even if you are cooking for one. You can then either freeze or refrigerate the rest for another meal. After all, who doesn't love having something pre-prepared and ready to go?

Our 'Many meals from one' pages explain how to cook up a big batch of beef stew, ratatouille or bolognese sauce, which you can then freeze in serving portions. The recipe then explains simple ways to transform these basic dishes into other tempting meals, so you are getting plenty of variety for little extra effort.

The 'Quick ideas' pages show you how to make the most of basic ingredients and add interest to meals. There are tricks for turning a simple soup into a memorable meal, ideas for speedy snacks, great pizza toppings, fillings for baked potatoes and ways to jazz up a steak.

Small is beautiful

Some ingredients — such as bacon, ham, salami and other preserved meats, cheeses, marinated vegetables and olives — can be bought by weight, rather than in packets and jars, so you can buy just the amount you need.

Many fruits and vegetables are also sold individually. This may cost a little more than buying larger quantities, but if you are not going to use it all up before it perishes, this is a false economy. Conveniently, salad and baby spinach leaves are also often sold loose or in bags.

Grow your own

If you have a garden, courtyard, balcony or windowbox, consider growing a few pots of your favourite herbs. This way you can pick and use as little as you need, rather than buying a whole bunch that never gets fully used, and enjoy absolute freshness. Leafy lettuce varieties are perfect too: you can pick off a few leaves as needed, without harvesting the whole plant.

Kitchen know-how

Your pantry, fridge and freezer are great kitchen allies when used to maximum effect. Add a few simple tips on versatile cookware and using up leftovers and you're on your way!

Pantry pals

Keep a few basic staples in the pantry so you can always whip up a tasty, nutritious and satisfying meal.

■ **Pasta, rice** and **couscous** keep well in airtight containers and quickly bulk up a meal.

■ **Canned fish** such as tuna, salmon and sardines are incredibly versatile and go well in salads, pasta dishes, omelettes and pizzas. They have a long shelf life, so are worth stocking up on when on sale.

■ **Canned legumes** including chickpeas, lentils and beans are great in soups, stews and salads. They are a wonderfully inexpensive protein source.

■ **Canned tomatoes** enrich soups, stews and sauces. Some already have added onion, garlic or herbs.

Clever cookware

If you are downscaling or just starting out, here are some great space and time savers.

■ A small hand-held stick blender can be placed straight into a hot pan of soup, so you don't have to tip all the soup into a blender or food processor or blender.

■ Simple hand-held electric beaters are fine for cake making and whipping cream. Unless you are a serious baker, you can probably do without a heavy, bulky stand-mixer.

■ A heatproof silicon spatula can be used for stir-frying, lifting and even folding ingredients.

■ A good flameproof casserole dish makes for one-pot cooking and serving. You can brown meat in it on top of the stove, then pop the same dish into the oven to finish the casserole off. The same dish can also be taken straight to the table for serving.

■ Forget about having a fancy array of knives: a large chef's knife, small paring knife and good bread knife are all you need.

■ A large, deep good-quality non-stick frying pan does triple duty as a frying pan, wok and simmering pot for stews and sauces. Cheap frying pans are a false economy as they scratch easily and don't last long.

Freezer favourites

Your freezer is a great asset when it comes to minimising waste. Just make sure everything is well sealed so it is airtight, and that you label and date packages for easy identification.

- Divide raw meat, fish or chicken into portions. Wrap tightly in plastic wrap, then place in a resealable bag and expel all the air. Whole steak and larger chicken portions will keep for up to 12 months; cubed meat for up to 6 months; and any type of minced (ground) meat for up to 3 months. Fish fillets will keep for up to 3 months. It is fine to refreeze meat if it was frozen raw, then thoroughly cooked in a recipe (such as steak used in a stew, or minced meat used in a bolognese sauce).

- Bread freezes well. Just make sure it is kept well-sealed, and expel as much air as possible each time you open it. To freeze unsliced bread, first cut it into slices of your desired thickness for easy retrieval.

- Sauces and pastes can be frozen in ice cube trays for easy portioning. Once frozen, transfer to an airtight resealable bag for easy access.

- Frozen berries are an inexpensive treat.

- Frozen peas, spinach and corn are so handy and nutritious. Add them to soups, stews or omelettes to boost your vegetable intake, or serve as a simple side dish.

Fridge friendly

Having an organised fridge will keep your food safe and appealing.

- Keep 'like' items together: dairy on the upper shelves, opened jars and condiments in the middle, and meat, fish or chicken on the lower shelves, where it is coldest.

- Always keep raw meat away from cooked foods, so there is no cross-contamination. Keep it in its packaging if well-sealed, or place on a plate and cover with plastic wrap. Stand it on a tray if there is any chance of it dripping onto other foods.

- Empty unused canned food portions into a sealed airtight container and refrigerate for up to 3 days.

- Keep perishable vegetables in the crisper.

Love your leftovers

Don't think of leftovers as a waste — imagine them as a whole new meal!

- Cooked pasta can be refrigerated for up to 3 days. To loosen it, place it in a heatproof bowl, cover with boiling water, stand for about a minute, then drain before reheating. You can add it soup, toss it into a quick salad with drained canned tuna, chopped tomatoes, capsicum (bell pepper) and rocket (arugula), or make a simple pasta bake by mixing it with a pasta sauce and any cooked chopped meat or chicken. Add thawed frozen peas and corn and sprinkle with cheese before baking.

- Leftover rice can be refrigerated for up to 2 days. It must be cooled and refrigerated as soon as possible after cooking, to avoid food poisoning. Rice reheats well in the microwave as a side dish, or work your own magic with our Brown fried rice recipe on page 60.

- Cooked vegetables are great in a frittata (see page 47). You can also mash them together and shape into patties; it is best to bind the mixture with a starchy vegetable such as potato, sweet potato or pumpkin (winter squash).

- Cooked meat is perfect on a sandwich. Also try it in little pies or pasties with some gravy or pasta sauce; these can be frozen for later use.

Starting the day

Breakfast is the most important meal of the day. Ideally it should contain a mix of fibre, protein, complex carbohydrates, vitamins and minerals to sustain you until lunchtime. Try these great ideas!

Great granola

Makes 8 serves

Preparation 15 minutes

Cooking 20 minutes

2 cups (200 g) rolled (porridge) oats
½ cup (60 g) chopped pecans
½ cup (70 g) pepitas (pumpkin seeds)
2 tablespoons maple syrup
1 tablespoon vegetable oil
¼ cup (15 g) shredded coconut
⅓ cup (50 g) diced dried apricots
⅓ cup (40 g) sultanas (golden raisins)

1 Preheat the oven to 180°C (350°F/Gas 4). Combine the oats, pecans and pepitas in a large bowl and make a well in the centre. Mix together the maple syrup and oil, then add to the dry ingredients and mix until coated.

2 Spread the mixture in a large roasting pan. Bake for 10 minutes, then remove from the oven. Stir and turn the mixture, then bake for a further 5 minutes. Stir in the coconut; cook for 5 minutes longer, or until the coconut is lightly golden.

3 Set aside to cool completely, stirring occasionally to release the heat. Mix in the apricots and sultanas and store in an airtight container. Serve with milk and fresh fruit.

Mix and match

Tailor-make your own granola and muesli, substituting the following ingredients, or using any combination you fancy.

Nuts and seeds Almonds, walnuts, pecans, hazelnuts (filberts), sesame seeds, sunflower seeds, linseeds (flax seeds) and pepitas (pumpkin seeds) contain healthy fats, vitamins and minerals to help you feel satisfied.

Grains Use any rolled grain, such as millet, rye and spelt, or a combination. Mixing it up adds variety and supplies different nutrients.

Dried fruit Try currants, raisins, sultanas (golden raisins), dates, apricots, goji berries and acai berries. Dried fruits are quite high in natural sugars, so use them in moderation.

Magic muesli

Makes 8 serves

2 cups (200 g) rolled (porridge) oats
½ cup (75 g) diced dried apricots
½ cup (60 g) slivered almonds
¼ cup (30 g) sunflower seeds
¼ cup (40 g) sesame seeds

Combine all the ingredients in a large bowl.
Mix well, then store in an airtight container.
Serve with milk and fresh fruit.

Brilliant bircher muesli

Makes 2 serves

1 cup (100 g) rolled (porridge) oats
½ cup (125 ml) apple juice
½ cup (125 g) low-fat natural (plain) yogurt
1 unpeeled, grated apple

Mix all the ingredients in a bowl; cover and
refrigerate overnight. To serve, mix with a little
extra yogurt, if desired; top with fresh fruit and
sprinkle with your favourite nuts and/or seeds.

Perfect porridge

Makes 2 serves

½ cup (50 g) rolled (porridge) oats
2 cups (500 ml) water

Place the ingredients in a small saucepan. Bring
to a boil, reduce the heat to low and simmer for
5 minutes, stirring regularly, until the oats have
thickened and are cooked through.

Serving ideas Sprinkle with **brown sugar** and
ground **cinnamon** or **chopped toasted nuts**.
Or top with **yogurt**, **fresh fruit** or **stewed fruit**
(see pages 220–221). To sweeten porridge
without using processed sugar, add **chopped
dried fruits** (such as dates) towards the end of
cooking; they will plump and soften.

Think outside the box

Check the label when buying cereal.
Make sure the sugar and saturated
fat levels are not too high, and be
aware that many commercial
cereals are quite high in salt.
Increase their nutritional value by
serving with fruit, nuts or seeds.

Excellent eggs

Poached, scrambled, boiled or fried, eggs served
with wholemeal (whole-wheat) toast are a highly
nutritious breakfast choice. For some great egg
ideas, see chapter 2, Snacks and light meals.

Tasty toasts

Nutrition-wise, wholegrain and wholemeal
(whole-wheat) breads are a better choice than
white bread. Sliced bread keeps well in the freezer
if tightly sealed, and can be toasted from frozen.

Great toast toppings

- Ripe avocado, sprinkled with a light squeeze
  of lemon juice.
- Reduced-fat cream cheese and ripe tomato.
- Protein-packed hot baked beans.
- Sliced button mushrooms, sautéed in a little
  olive oil until soft, with a little fresh or dried
  thyme; you can also fry them with some
  halved cherry tomatoes if you like.
- Spread toasted fruit bread with ricotta or
  reduced-fat cream cheese, top with sliced
  banana and serve drizzled with a little honey.

noodles Quick ideas to... turn soup into a meal Easy min

Easy minestrone CHILLED LEEK SOUP STEP-BY-STEP Hear

uick ideas to... turn soup into a meal Minted asparagus an

leek soup Step-by-step Speedy bouillabaisse Chicken noo

UICK IDEAS TO... TURN SOUP INTO A MEAL Miso

Miso soup with tofu and noodles Chilled leek sou

aragus and pea soup MINTED ASPARAGUS AND PEA

Hearty potato soup Chicken noodle soup Spee

soups

Minted asparagus and pea soup

For 2

Preparation 10 minutes

- -

Cooking 15 minutes

Quick

One-pot

1 bunch (175 g/6 oz) asparagus

2 teaspoons olive oil

1 French shallot, chopped

1 potato (100 g/3½ oz), peeled and diced into small cubes

2 cups (500 ml) vegetable stock

4 fresh mint leaves

½ cup (80 g) frozen peas

2 tablespoons thick (Greek-style) yogurt

2 tablespoons toasted pine nuts

- -

Each serving (1½ cups) provides
1147 kJ, 247 kcal, 10 g protein, 18 g fat
(3 g saturated fat), 19 g carbohydrate
(9 g sugars), 3 g fibre, 1046 mg sodium

1 Trim the woody ends from the asparagus spears. Cut off and reserve the tender tips, then roughly chop the stems.

2 Heat the oil in a saucepan over medium heat. Add the shallot, chopped asparagus stems and potato. Cover and cook, stirring occasionally, for 6–8 minutes, or until tender.

3 Add the stock, mint and most of the peas, reserving about 1–2 tablespoons of peas. Cook for 2–3 minutes, then allow the soup to cool slightly. Process to a smooth purée using a hand-held stick blender. Season with salt and freshly ground black pepper.

4 Bring the soup back to a boil, then stir in the reserved asparagus tips and peas. Cook for 2 minutes, or until the asparagus and peas are just tender.

5 Serve with a swirl of yogurt, scattered with the pine nuts.

Leftover magic

Instead of a fresh potato, you could add about ¼ cup (55 g) leftover mashed potato or cooked rice to the soup during the last few minutes of cooking.

Cook's tip

To toast pine nuts, place them in a small, dry frying pan and stir over medium–high heat for 1 minute, or until lightly golden.

This lovely soup makes great use of fresh asparagus. It will keep for a day or two, so it is worth making two serves, even if cooking for one. Try it with our Ricotta and pesto bites (page 30).

Here's a great use for leftover roast or barbecue chicken. You can also use thinly sliced fresh chicken breast: simmer it in the stock in step 2 until cooked through.

Chicken noodle soup

Preparation 15 minutes

Cooking 10 minutes

For 1

1 teaspoon olive oil
½ small brown onion, diced
½ carrot, diced
½ celery stalk, diced
1 cup (250 ml) chicken stock
½ an 85 g (3 oz) packet of
    2-minute noodles
½ cup (85 g) shredded or chopped
    cooked chicken meat
chopped fresh parsley, to garnish

For 2

2 teaspoons olive oil
1 small brown onion, diced
1 carrot, diced
1 celery stalk, diced
2 cups (500 ml) chicken stock
85 g (3 oz) packet of 2-minute
    noodles
1 cup (175 g) shredded or chopped
    cooked chicken meat
chopped fresh parsley, to garnish

1 Heat the oil in a saucepan over medium heat. Add the onion, carrot and celery and cook for 5 minutes, or until tender. Pour in the stock and 2 cups (500 ml) water and bring to a boil.

2 Break up the noodles while they're still in the packet, then add to the soup with the chicken meat. Cook for 2 minutes, or until the noodles are tender and the chicken is heated through. Serve immediately.

Each serving provides
2380 kJ, 568 kcal, 33 g protein, 26 g fat (10 g saturated fat), 51 g carbohydrate (5 g sugars), 8 g fibre, 1273 mg sodium

Serving suggestion

Garnish with chopped fresh parsley.

Other ideas

■ Add a pinch of mixed dried Mediterranean herbs with the stock.

▨ Instead of 2-minute noodles, use vermicelli, rice noodles, egg noodles or udon noodles, and flavour the soup with South-East Asian herbs and spices, such as fresh ginger, fresh chilli and coriander (cilantro).

Cook's tip

Leftover noodles can be sealed in the packet with a rubber band and kept in an airtight container in the pantry until required.

Chilled leek soup

Preparation 15 minutes
+ 2 hours chilling
- -
Cooking 25 minutes

For 2

2 teaspoons butter

1 leek, white part only, thinly
sliced

1 celery stalk, finely sliced

2 potatoes (300 g/10 oz), peeled
and chopped

2 cups (500 ml) chicken stock

⅓ cup (80 ml) pouring cream

ground white pepper, to taste

1 tablespoon snipped fresh chives

- -

Each serving provides
1315 kJ, 314 kcal, 9 g protein, 19 g fat
(12 g saturated fat), 26 g carbohydrate
(7 g sugars), 4 g fibre, 703 mg sodium

Leftover magic

- Leftover leek can be used in the
Speedy bouillabaisse on page 28.
- Celery can be purchased by the stalk
from many supermarkets; any leftover
celery can be used in salads or in the
Easy minestrone on page 24.

Cook's tip

This soup is a version of vichyssoise
which is traditionally served chilled but if
you're in a hurry, it is also delicious hot.

Step 1 Melt the butter in a saucepan over low heat. Add the leek and celery. Cook, stirring occasionally without browning, for 5–6 minutes, or until soft.

Step 2 Add the potato and stock. Bring to a boil, then reduce the heat and simmer for 15 minutes, or until the potato is very soft. Allow to cool for 20 minutes, then purée the soup using a hand-held stick blender.

Step 3 Stir in half the cream and season with salt and white pepper. Transfer to a bowl, cover with plastic wrap and chill for at least 2 hours. Serve drizzled with the remaining cream and sprinkled with chives. Without the cream, the soup can be frozen for several months.

Hearty potato soup

Preparation 10 minutes

Cooking 20 minutes

For 1

1 teaspoon olive oil

1 potato (150 g/5 oz), peeled and chopped

½ small onion, chopped

1 small clove garlic, crushed

1½ cups (375 ml) vegetable stock

¾ cup (85 g) small cauliflower florets

½ small carrot, sliced

¼ cup (30 g) sliced green beans

½ cup (25 g) baby English spinach leaves

For 2

2 teaspoons olive oil

2 potatoes (300 g/10 oz), peeled and chopped

1 small onion, chopped

1 clove garlic, crushed

3 cups (750 ml) vegetable stock

1½ cups (170 g) small cauliflower florets

1 small carrot, sliced

½ cup (60 g) sliced green beans

1 cup (50 g) baby English spinach leaves

1 Heat the oil in a saucepan over medium heat. Add the potato and onion and cook, stirring occasionally, for 5 minutes, or until the potato starts to soften. Add the garlic in the last minute.

2 Pour in the stock and add the cauliflower. Bring to a boil, reduce the heat and simmer for 10 minutes.

3 Add the carrot and beans and simmer for a further 5 minutes, or until the vegetables are cooked. Remove from the heat, stir in the spinach and serve.

Each serving provides
923 kJ, 221 kcal, 8 g protein, 6 g fat (1 g saturated fat), 32 g carbohydrate (12 g sugars), 6 g fibre, 1578 mg sodium

Serving suggestion

The soup is delicious with **grilled cheesy toasts**: cut half a baguette stick into thick diagonal slices and lay a slice of brie on each. Place under a hot grill (broiler) and cook until the cheese melts. Serve with a teaspoon of pesto on top.

Cook's tips

- This soup doesn't freeze very well, but leftovers can be refrigerated for several days.

- Frozen green beans are convenient and nutritious and can be used instead of fresh beans in this soup. There is no need to thaw them first.

Easy minestrone

Preparation 15 minutes

- -

Cooking 20 minutes

For 1

1 teaspoon olive oil

1 small slice rindless bacon (bacon strip), chopped

½ small onion, chopped

½ stick celery, chopped

1 small clove garlic, crushed

1 cup (250 ml) beef stock

2 teaspoons red wine

1 small roma (plum) tomato, chopped

1 small carrot, chopped

1 tablespoon risoni pasta

1 tablespoon frozen peas

half a 125 g (4 oz) can red kidney beans, rinsed and drained

1 teaspoon chopped fresh parsley

2 teaspoons bottled pesto

2 teaspoons finely grated parmesan

For 2

2 teaspoons olive oil

1 large slice rindless bacon (bacon strip), chopped

1 small onion, chopped

1 stick celery, chopped

1 clove garlic, crushed

2 cups (500 ml) beef stock

1 tablespoon red wine

1 roma (plum) tomato, chopped

1 small carrot, chopped

¼ cup (60 g) risoni pasta

2 tablespoons frozen peas

125 g (4 oz) can red kidney beans, rinsed and drained

2 teaspoons chopped fresh parsley

1 tablespoon bottled pesto

1 tablespoon finely grated parmesan

Each serving provides
1431 kJ, 342 kcal, 26 g protein, 15 g fat (4 g saturated fat), 24 g carbohydrate (9 g sugars), 6 g fibre, 1966 mg sodium

Leftover magic

- Leftover risoni can be used in our **Risoni hotpot** (page 198).

- If you have any leftover cooked pasta, omit the risoni and add your pasta to the soup in the last minute of cooking to warm it through.

- Refrigerate leftover canned beans in an airtight container and use in soups, salads or nachos.

1 Heat the oil in a saucepan and cook the bacon, onion, celery and garlic over medium heat for 5 minutes, or until the vegetables have softened and the bacon is golden.

2 Add the stock, wine, tomato and carrot. Bring to a boil and simmer for 5 minutes. Stir in the risoni and simmer for a further 6 minutes, stirring occasionally.

3 Add the peas and beans and simmer for 4 minutes. Remove from the heat and stir in the parsley. Serve with a swirl of pesto and a sprinkling of parmesan.

Leftover magic

- Leftover noodles can be used in our **Chicken noodle soup** (page 19), as well as noodle salads and stir-fries.
- Nori (thin sheets of dried seaweed) will keep well and can be used in sushi.
- Miso paste can be refrigerated in an airtight container for up to 6 months.

Cook's tips

- White miso paste is milder than the red.
- Dashi is a Japanese fish-flavoured stock (bouillon) powder. Watered-down chicken stock can be used instead — $\frac{1}{2}$ cup (125 ml) chicken stock with $\frac{1}{2}$ cup (125 ml) water per person.
- Do not boil the soup after the miso paste has been added, as this destroys the miso's health-giving properties.

Miso soup with tofu and noodles

Preparation 10 minutes

Cooking 10 minutes + 2 minutes standing

For 1

1 teaspoon vegetable oil

1 teaspoon finely grated fresh ginger

½ small onion, thinly sliced

½ carrot, sliced

50 g (1¾ oz) button mushrooms, sliced

½ teaspoon dashi powder

110 g (3½ oz) shelf-fresh udon noodles

50 g (1¾ oz) firm tofu, cut into cubes

1 tablespoon white miso paste

a few drops of sesame oil

½ spring onion (scallion), sliced

shredded nori, to garnish (optional)

For 2

2 teaspoons vegetable oil

2 teaspoons finely grated fresh ginger

1 small onion, thinly sliced

1 carrot, sliced

100 g (3½ oz) button mushrooms, sliced

1 teaspoon dashi powder

220 g (8 oz) shelf-fresh udon noodles

100 g (3½ oz) firm tofu, cut into cubes

2 tablespoons white miso paste

a few drops of sesame oil

1 spring onion (scallion), sliced

shredded nori, to garnish (optional)

1 Heat the vegetable oil in a saucepan over medium heat. Add the ginger and vegetables and cook for 1 minute, or until slightly softened.

2 Mix the dashi with 1½ cups (375 ml) water per person, then add to the pan. Bring to a boil, reduce the heat and simmer for 3–4 minutes, or until the vegetables are cooked.

3 Add the noodles and separate with a fork. Add the tofu and simmer for 1 minute, then turn off the heat.

4 Scoop out ¼ cup (60 ml) of the dashi broth, then stir the miso into the broth to make a loose paste. Stir the miso broth through the soup with the sesame oil. Cover and let stand for 2 minutes.

5 Serve immediately, sprinkled with the spring onion, and a little shredded nori if desired.

Each serving provides
1292 kJ, 309 kcal, 12 g protein, 10 g fat (1 g saturated fat), 42 g carbohydrate (3 g sugars), 3 g fibre, 265 mg sodium

Speedy bouillabaisse

Preparation 10 minutes

Cooking 15 minutes

For 1

2 teaspoons olive oil

½ small red onion, sliced

½ small leek, white part only, thinly sliced

1 small clove garlic, crushed

half a 410 g (15 oz) can chopped tomatoes

¾ cup (180 ml) fish or vegetable stock

150 g (5 oz) seafood marinara mix

For 2

1 tablespoon olive oil

1 small red onion, sliced

1 small leek, white part only, thinly sliced

1 clove garlic, crushed

410 g (15 oz) can chopped tomatoes

1½ cups (375 ml) fish or vegetable stock

300 g (10 oz) seafood marinara mix

1 Heat the oil in a saucepan over medium heat. Add the onion, leek and garlic and cook for 5 minutes, or until softened.

2 Pour in the tomatoes and stock. Bring to a boil, reduce the heat and simmer for 3 minutes.

3 Add the marinara mix, then cover and simmer for 4–5 minutes, or until the seafood is cooked through. Serve immediately.

Serving suggestions

Stir chopped fresh parsley through the soup just before serving, or garnish with basil leaves. Serve with crusty bread and lemon or lime wedges.

Leftover magic

Use any leftover canned tomatoes in our **Easy minestrone** (page 24) instead of fresh tomato, and in tomato-based sauces and stews.

Each serving provides
1368 kJ, 327 kcal, 35 g protein, 15 g fat (3 g saturated fat), 14 g carbohydrate (12 g sugars), 5 g fibre, 1181 mg sodium

Cook's tip

Most supermarkets and fishmongers will sell you as much or as little marinara mix as you need. Instead, you can also use boneless firm white fish fillets, cut into bite-sized pieces, or any seafood you like.

Quick ideas to... turn **soup** into a meal

Some soups make a hearty meal. Others need an extra 'something' — a bit of protein, a carbohydrate element or something fresh and green — to round them out. Here are a few tricks to bowl you over.

Carbs and crunch

Hummus fingers

Toast some thinly sliced **pide (Turkish flat bread)** under a hot grill (broiler) until golden brown on both sides. Spread generously with ready-made **hummus** and drizzle with **extra virgin olive oil.**

Tapenade toasts

Toast slices of **sourdough bread** under a hot grill (broiler) until golden on both sides. Spread with ready-made **tapenade (olive paste)** and top with **sliced tomato.**

Ricotta & pesto bites

Cut a **baguette** into 1 cm (½ inch) slices and toast under a hot grill (broiler) until golden on both sides. Spread with ready-made **pesto** and **fresh ricotta,** then grill (broil) until the ricotta is lightly golden.

Crunchy croutons

Cut or tear **day-old bread** into 2 cm (¾ inch) pieces. Heat 1 cm (½ inch) **olive oil** in a small frying pan over medium–high heat. Fry the bread until crisp and golden brown, then drain on paper towels. Alternatively, spread the bread on a baking tray, spray with a little olive oil spray and bake in a preheated 190°C (375°F/Gas 5) oven for 5–10 minutes, or until crisp and golden.

More **easy** carb ideas

- Add cooked pasta to your hot soup. Any type is fine, but you may want to break up long pasta. Cook the pasta separately first so it doesn't absorb too much of the liquid in the soup.

- Stir some leftover cooked rice into the soup. Brown rice is particularly good as it keeps its shape and texture.

- Add rice noodles, such as flat rice-stick noodles or rice vermicelli. Simply soak them in boiling water for 5 minutes, then drain and add to the hot soup.

Protein power

- Canned beans, lentils and chickpeas add a satisfying, healthy element to any meal. Stir them directly into the soup, or make a quick accompanying salad by combining them with chopped spring onion (scallion), tomatoes and baby English spinach leaves, then drizzling with extra virgin olive oil and a little red wine vinegar or lemon juice.

- Canned tuna is a great pantry stand-by, and comes in convenient individual-serve sizes. It can be added to soup at the last minute, to gently heat through.

- Chopped ham, shredded leftover chicken, or any type of leftover cooked meat can be added to soup. Just cut it into small pieces and add to your hot soup — it will heat through quickly.

- Serve your soup sprinkled with grated firm cheese such as cheddar or parmesan, or try crumbling soft cheeses such as fetta, ricotta or even a mild blue over the soup.

- Eggs can be added to soups in many ways. You could chop up boiled eggs to sprinkle on top, or cook them omelette-style (see page 36) and cut into pieces. Or add a lightly beaten raw egg to hot soup in a thin stream, stirring constantly — the egg will cook as it hits the hot liquid.

Fresh and fabulous

Leafy greens should be included in a meal whenever possible, and you can always serve a simple salad before or after your soup. Another way to increase the green quotient is to add chopped spinach, silverbeet (Swiss chard), kale or mustard greens to the hot soup; they will cook quickly in the heat.

Remember that adding a squeeze of lemon or lime juice will help your body to absorb the iron present in leafy greens, and will also add a fresh zing of flavour.

Try these ideas

- Add chopped Asian greens. The stems take a little longer to cook, so chop them separately and briefly cook before adding the leaves.

- Broccoli is full of goodness. Chop it into small florets and cook for only about 5 minutes in the soup, so it still has some texture.

- Some greens can be added at the table to simply wilt into the hot soup, rather than having to be cooked. Try a good handful of chopped or baby rocket (arugula), watercress sprigs, or baby English spinach leaves.

- Think of fresh herbs as salad leaves, rather than something to be added in tiny pinches. Herbs such as flat-leaf (Italian) parsley, basil, coriander (cilantro) and chervil will add lovely fresh flavours, either alone, or even in a mixture.

Quick ideas for... pizza   Grilled mushrooms on cia

fried rice   SCRAMBLED EGGS WITH SMOKED SALMON   ste

ideas for...baked jacket potatoes   Baked egg pots   Brown

ed egg pots   Fruit smoothie   Quesadilla

UICK IDEAS FOR...   SPEEDY SNACKS   Croque monsieur

Omelette Step-by-step   Salmon fish cake   Mini f

Eggs florentine   BEAN TORTILLA BASKET   Cheese souf

chicken fajitas   Colcannon   Fresh rice paper rolls   Che

snacks and light meals

Fruit smoothie

Preparation 5 minutes

Cooking None

Quick

No-Cook

For 1

½ cup (125 ml) low-fat milk

1 small ripe banana or mango

2 tablespoons fresh or frozen
blueberries or strawberries

½ teaspoon honey, or to taste

For 2

1 cup (250 ml) low-fat milk

1 ripe banana or mango

¼ cup (40 g) fresh or frozen
blueberries or strawberries

1 teaspoon honey, or to taste

1 Combine all the ingredients in a blender and blend until smooth.

2 Pour into glasses and serve.

Each serving provides
516 kJ, 123 kcal, 7 g protein, <1 g fat (<1 g saturated fat), 24 g carbohydrate (22 g sugars), 1 g fibre, 76 mg sodium

Other ideas

- For a high-protein smoothie, add ¼ cup (60 g) silken tofu (for 1), or ½ cup (125 g) silken tofu (for 2); alternatively, add an egg, if raw eggs aren't an issue for you.
- Replace the milk with soy, oat or rice milk.
- Instead of milk, use low-fat fruit-flavoured yogurt — or a mix of fruit juice and natural (plain) yogurt.
- You can use dried fruits (apricots, pitted prunes or dates), but you may need to soften them first by soaking or gently simmering them in water.
- Add a pinch of spice, such as ground nutmeg, cinnamon or ginger.
- For added nutrients, extra options include protein supplement powders, wheat germ, linseeds (flax seeds), LSA (ground linseeds, sunflowers and almonds), and soft nuts such as walnuts or pecans.

Cook's tip

You can use any fresh or frozen soft fruit that purées easily in a blender, such as pears, melon, pitted cherries, papaya or pawpaw, avocado, kiwi fruit and passionfruit. Canned fruits are also fine — these keep well in the pantry, and are often sold in small tubs.

Omelette

Preparation 5 minutes

Cooking 5 minutes

For 1

2–3 eggs (depending on how
    hungry you are)

1 tablespoon milk or water
    (milk gives a fluffier result)

1 teaspoon butter

1 slice of toast, to serve

tomato chutney, to serve

basil leaves, to garnish

Each serving provides
1093 kJ, 261 kcal, 20 g protein, 20 g fat
(8 g saturated fat), 1 g carbohydrate
(1 g sugars), 0 g fibre, 242 mg sodium

Making an omelette
is an easy skill to master.
The freshest eggs will give the
best result. If you're cooking for
two people, it's better to make
two single omelettes than one
big one — the omelettes will
be easier to handle.

Step 1 Gently crack the eggs into a bowl. Add the milk or water and a pinch of salt and freshly ground black pepper, then lightly beat together with a fork. Be careful not to overbeat the eggs or they will become tough.

Step 2 Heat a 15 cm (6 inch) non-stick frying pan over medium–high heat. Add the butter and swirl the pan until it foams. Immediately pour in the eggs and cook for 20 seconds, or until the omelette starts to set around the edges. Using a fork or spatula, gently pull the edges of the cooked egg into the middle of the omelette, tilting the pan so the runny bits run onto the hot pan.

When the egg is creamy on top and golden underneath, flip one half of the omelette over the other, into a neat semi-circle. Place the toast on a warmed plate and slide the omelette onto the toast. Spread tomato chutney on the omelette, fold over, and top with basil leaves. Serve immediately.

Other ideas

- Try any of your favourite cheeses in the omelette. If using a soft cheese such as brie or camembert, add it to the omelette just before you place it under the grill (broiler) or it will dissolve.

- Sprinkle the omelette with chopped ham, prosciutto or shredded cooked chicken just before it goes under the grill.

Cheese soufflé omelette

Preparation 10 minutes

Cooking 2 minutes (for 1), 4 minutes (for 2)

For 1

3 eggs

ground white pepper, to taste

1 tablespoon chopped fresh
    parsley or herb of your choice

½ tablespoon butter

1 tablespoon grated gruyère

1 tablespoon grated cheddar

For 2

6 eggs

ground white pepper, to taste

2 tablespoons chopped fresh
    parsley or herb of your choice

1 tablespoon butter

2 tablespoons grated gruyère

2 tablespoons grated cheddar

1 Preheat the grill (broiler) to medium–high.

2 Separate the eggs, placing the eggwhites in a very clean bowl. In a small bowl, beat the yolks until well combined, then season with salt and ground white pepper.

3 Using a balloon whisk or electric beaters, whisk the eggwhites until soft peaks form. Lightly fold the egg yolks, parsley and cheeses through.

4 Place a heavy-based 20 cm (8 inch) frying pan over medium–low heat if cooking for one; if cooking for two, use a 23–24 cm (9–9½ inch) pan. Melt the butter in the pan, then swirl the butter around the pan and slightly up the side. Spoon the egg mixture into the pan, covering the base. Cook for 1 minute, or 2 minutes if making an omelette for two.

5 Place the pan under the hot grill, then cook the omelette until the egg is just set and lightly golden — about 1 minute if cooking for one, or 2 minutes if cooking for two.

6 Carefully run a pallet knife or flat knife around the edge of the omelette to loosen it. Slide half the omelette onto a plate, then flip the other half over into a neat semi-circle and serve.

Serving suggestion

Lovely with a simple side salad and hot buttered wholegrain or wholemeal (whole-wheat) toast.

Each serving provides
1513 kJ, 361 kcal, 25 g protein, 30 g fat (13 g saturated fat), <1 g carbohydrate (<1 g sugars), <1 g fibre, 365 mg sodium

Baked egg pots

Preparation 5 minutes

Cooking 15 minutes

For 1

2 tablespoons tomato pasta
   sauce

1 thin slice ham, chopped

1 egg

1 teaspoon chopped fresh
   parsley or chives

For 2

4 tablespoons tomato pasta
   sauce

2 thin slices ham, chopped

2 eggs

2 teaspoons chopped fresh
   parsley or chives

Each serving provides
526 kJ, 126 kcal, 12 g protein, 6 g fat (2 g saturated fat),
5 g carbohydrate (3 g sugars), 1 g fibre, 609 mg sodium

1 Preheat the oven to 180°C (350°F/Gas 4).
Lightly grease one or two ½ cup (125 ml)
ramekins or ovenproof dishes.

2 Spoon the pasta sauce into each ramekin
and sprinkle the ham over the top. Stand the
ramekin or ramekins on a baking tray, then
carefully crack an egg into each one, taking care
not to break the yolk.

3 Bake for 15 minutes, or until the eggwhite
is just set but the yolk is still a little runny.

4 Sprinkle with the parsley or chives and serve
immediately, as the egg will continue to cook.

Serving suggestion

To make the most of your hot oven, put in
some bread slices to toast at the same time.
For a simple side dish you could also bake some
cherry tomatoes, fresh asparagus spears or small
mushroom caps; give them a drizzle of olive oil
and season lightly before baking.

Cook's tip

This is a great way to use leftover tomato pasta
sauce. A spicy tomato pasta sauce, such as an
Italian-style arrabiata, is especially good.

Other ideas

- Replace the ham with prosciutto or lean
  cooked bacon, and add some leftover canned
  corn kernels.
- Instead of tomato pasta sauce, use your
  favourite chutney or a spicy salsa.

Baking eggs in individual ramekins makes them look special and easy to serve. They are also very simple to prepare.

Eggs florentine

Preparation 10 minutes

Cooking 5 minutes

For 1

butter, for greasing and spreading

75 g (2½ oz) frozen spinach, thawed

1 egg

1 slice sourdough bread

1 tablespoon cream cheese

1 tablespoon grated cheddar

¼ teaspoon dijon mustard

For 2

butter, for greasing and spreading

150 g (5 oz) frozen spinach, thawed

2 eggs

2 slices sourdough bread

2 tablespoons cream cheese

2 tablespoons grated cheddar

½ teaspoon dijon mustard

1 Place a frying pan with a lid over high heat. Half-fill it with water and bring to a simmer.

2 Lightly grease one or two ¾ cup (180 ml) ramekins with butter. Squeeze any excess water out of the spinach, then spread the spinach over the base of the ramekin and part way up the side to make a nest. Crack an egg into each ramekin and season with salt and freshly ground black pepper. Place the ramekins in the simmering hot water. Cover with the lid and steam for 4–5 minutes, or until the eggwhite is set.

3 Meanwhile, lightly toast the bread. In a small bowl, combine the cream cheese, cheddar and mustard.

4 To serve, carefully remove the ramekins from the pan and place on individual plates. Dollop with a heaped tablespoon of the cream cheese mixture and serve with the hot buttered toast.

Another idea

Add some finely chopped fresh herbs or ham to the cream cheese mixture.

Cook's tips

- You can buy frozen spinach in packets of small blocks, making it easy and convenient to cook small quantities.

- Put any leftover bread in a food processor and make breadcrumbs. They freeze well and can be used for stuffings, toppings or crumbing.

Each serving provides
1129 kJ, 279 kcal, 14 g protein, 17 g fat (9 g saturated fat), 13 g carbohydrate (2 g sugars), 1 g fibre, 419 mg sodium

Scrambled eggs with smoked salmon

Preparation 5 minutes

Cooking 5 minutes

For 1

2 eggs

1½ tablespoons milk

ground white pepper, to taste

1 teaspoon butter, plus extra for spreading (optional)

1 wholemeal (whole-wheat) English muffin, split in half and toasted

50 g (1¾ oz) smoked salmon

1 teaspoon chopped chives, to serve

For 2

4 eggs

¼ cup (60 ml) milk

ground white pepper, to taste

1 teaspoon butter, plus extra for spreading (optional)

2 wholemeal (whole-wheat) English muffins, split in half and toasted

100 g (3½ oz) smoked salmon

2 teaspoons chopped chives, to serve

Each serving provides
1557 kJ, 372 kcal, 33 g protein, 16 g fat
(6 g saturated fat), 23 g carbohydrate
(3 g sugars), 3 g fibre, 1292 mg sodium

Step 1 Break the eggs into a small bowl. Add the milk and season with a pinch of ground white pepper. Lightly whisk to combine, until the mixture is pale yellow.

Step 2 Melt the butter in a medium frying pan over medium heat. When the butter is bubbling, pour in the eggs.

Step 3 Using a wooden spoon, gently scrape the eggs from the outside of the pan to the centre, until they start to set — about 1 minute for 2 eggs and slightly longer for 4 eggs. When the eggs are still a bit runny, remove the pan from the heat and lightly scramble with a fork for 10–15 seconds; the eggs will continue to cook off the heat. Serve on the muffins. Top with smoked salmon and chopped chives. Season to taste.

If three frittatas are too much for you, cover and refrigerate the leftovers and enjoy them the next day, sliced in a crusty baguette.

Mini frittatas

Preparation 5 minutes

Cooking 25 minutes

For 1

1 teaspoon olive oil

2 slices rindless bacon (bacon strips), roughly chopped

1 spring onion (scallion), sliced

2 tablespoons frozen peas

2 eggs

2 tablespoons milk

1½ tablespoons grated parmesan

For 2

2 teaspoons olive oil

4 slices rindless bacon (bacon strips), roughly chopped

2 spring onions (scallions), sliced

⅓ cup (50 g) frozen peas

4 eggs

⅓ cup (80 ml) milk

¼ cup (25 g) grated parmesan

Each serving provides
2165 kJ, 517 kcal, 46 g protein, 34 g fat (12 g saturated fat), 7 g carbohydrate (5 g sugars), <1 g fibre, 1682 mg sodium

1 Preheat the oven to 200°C (400°F/Gas 6). Heat the oil in a frying pan over medium–high heat, then fry the bacon for 3 minutes, or until crisp. Add the spring onion and cook for 1 minute; add the frozen peas and stir until thawed. Remove from the heat and allow to cool.

2 Whisk the eggs, milk and cheese in a bowl with some sea salt and freshly ground black pepper until combined. Stir the cooled bacon mixture through.

3 Using a standard muffin tin, lightly grease three holes per person. Spoon the mixture (about ¼ cup per muffin) into the muffin holes and bake for 18–20 minutes, or until the frittatas are golden and set.

Serving suggestion

Serve hot or cold, with a light salad of baby cos (romaine) lettuce, thinly sliced cucumber and parmesan shavings.

Other ideas

Try these lovely flavour combinations:

- canned tuna and frozen sweet corn
- sliced button mushrooms and diced tomato
- thawed frozen spinach, mixed with crumbled fetta cheese.

Cook's tip

You can buy bacon by the slice from many delicatessen counters.

Grilled mushrooms on ciabatta

Preparation 10 minutes

Cooking 10 minutes

For 1

150 g (5 oz) flat mushrooms
½ teaspoon chopped fresh thyme
½ teaspoon snipped fresh chives
1 teaspoon olive oil
2 slices ciabatta bread
¼ cup (35 g) crumbled soft fetta
¼ lemon

For 2

300 g (10 oz) flat mushrooms
1 teaspoon chopped fresh thyme
1 teaspoon snipped fresh chives
2 teaspoons olive oil
4 slices ciabatta bread
½ cup (75 g) crumbled soft fetta
½ lemon

1 Preheat the grill (broiler) to very high.

2 Trim the mushroom stems, leaving most of the stem intact. Place the mushrooms stem side up on a baking tray. Sprinkle with the thyme and chives, then drizzle with the oil. Grill (broil) for 3 minutes, then turn the mushrooms over and cook for a further 3 minutes.

3 Meanwhile, lightly toast the bread.

4 Place the cooked mushrooms on top of the toast, then sprinkle with the fetta. Squeeze some lemon juice over and serve.

Serving suggestion

Enjoy as a quick light meal with a simple side salad or mashed potato — or for a more substantial meal, serve the mushrooms on top of a steak, or with your favourite sausages.

Other ideas

Include some finely sliced garlic, a sprinkling of grated parmesan or some toasted pine nuts in the mushroom topping.

Each serving provides
1240 kJ, 296 kcal, 16 g protein, 15 g fat (6 g saturated fat), 24 g carbohydrate (1 g sugars), 5 g fibre, 643 mg sodium

Cook's tips

Try using other varieties of
mushrooms for this recipe, such as
portobello or pine mushrooms.

Fetta cheese that is sold in oil will keep
in the fridge for several months.

Leftover magic

Use any leftover sourdough bread in the **Panzanella salad** on page 84. Alternatively, place the bread in a food processor and make some breadcrumbs — these freeze well and can be used for stuffings, toppings or crumbing.

Other ideas

- Turn a 'croque monsieur' into a 'croque madame' by serving a fried egg on top.
- Try an Italian twist — replace the ham with salami and the Swiss cheese with mozzarella; use ciabatta bread and add some basil leaves.

Croque monsieur

Preparation 10 minutes

Cooking 10 minutes (for 1), 13 minutes (for 2)

For 1

3 teaspoons butter, plus
  2 teaspoons extra

½ tablespoon plain (all-purpose)
  flour

¼ cup (60 ml) milk

1 tablespoon grated parmesan

½ teaspoon dijon mustard

2 slices sourdough bread

50 g (1¾ oz) sliced ham

1 slice Swiss cheese

For 2

1½ tablespoons butter, plus
  1 tablespoon extra

1 tablespoon plain (all-purpose)
  flour

½ cup (125 ml) milk

2 tablespoons grated parmesan

1 teaspoon dijon mustard

4 slices sourdough bread

100 g (3½ oz) sliced ham

2 slices Swiss cheese

1 Preheat the grill (broiler) to high.

2 Melt the butter in a small saucepan over medium heat. Stir in the flour to make a thick paste, then gradually add the milk, stirring until smooth. Increase the heat to high and stir for another 30–60 seconds, or until the sauce is thick and smooth. Stir in the parmesan to make a béchamel sauce, then set aside.

3 Spread the mustard over half the bread slices, then top each with 50 g (1¾ oz) ham and a cheese slice. Top with the remaining bread to make a sandwich.

4 Place a small frying pan over medium heat. Melt the remaining butter (or half the remaining butter if making two sandwiches) in the hot pan. Fry one sandwich for 1 minute on each side, or until golden all over, then place on a baking tray.

If making two sandwiches, melt the remaining butter in the pan and fry the second sandwich as before.

5 Spread the béchamel sauce over the top of the sandwich or sandwiches. Place under the grill for 4–5 minutes, or until the béchamel is golden and bubbling. Serve hot.

Serving suggestion

Lovely with fresh mixed leaves or a simple garden salad.

Each serving provides
2242 kJ, 536 kcal, 25 g protein, 35 g fat (21 g saturated fat), 30 g carbohydrate (5 g sugars), 2 g fibre, 1470 mg sodium

Sometimes you just want a simple but appetising snack to tide
you over. Enjoy these snappy bites on their own, with a simple salad,
or even with a bowl of soup for a more substantial meal.

Best-ever bruschetta

Cut thick slices from a good sourdough or
rustic-style loaf of bread. (If the loaf is narrow,
cut it diagonally to give more surface area for
the topping.) Toast the bread on both sides until
golden brown. Rub the top of each toast with
a cut garlic clove, then drizzle with extra virgin
olive oil. Top with one of the following toppings
and serve immediately.

Classic tomato and basil

Mix together some finely diced ripe **tomato**
and fresh shredded **basil**, then season with
salt and freshly ground black pepper.

Classic plus

Add some canned **white beans** to the Classic
tomato and basil mixture above, along with a
sliced **spring onion** (scallion) and a drizzle of
balsamic vinegar. Or top the tomato and basil
mixture with canned **sardines**, some finely sliced

red onion and a few **capers**. Alternatively,
spread the bruschetta with ready-made basil
pesto, add some chopped pitted **olives** and
parsley to the tomato and basil mixture and
spoon it onto the bruschetta.

More topping ideas

- Top the bruschetta with an antipasto mix
  of chargrilled or marinated vegetables,
  such as eggplant (aubergine), mushroom,
  zucchini (courgette) and capsicum (bell
  pepper). Add sliced prosciutto if you like.

- Spread with ricotta or cream cheese and
  top with smoked salmon. Sprinkle with
  fresh chives and a squeeze of lemon juice.

- Top with flaked canned tuna and some
  cherry tomatoes that have been sautéed
  with a crushed garlic clove in a little olive oil.

- Boil broad (fava) beans until tender;
  drain and slip off the skins. Mash roughly
  with olive oil and lemon juice. Spread on
  the bruschetta and crumble fetta over.

- Spread the bruschetta with hummus and
  top with finely diced ripe tomato mixed
  with chopped fresh coriander (cilantro).

Magical melts

Cheese on toast doesn't have to be boring with these hot ideas. First toast some bread slices on both sides for a crunchy base, then add one of the following toppings, being sure to drain any wet ingredients. Cook under a hot grill (broiler) until the cheese is golden brown and bubbling. Keep a close watch, as the melts cook quickly!

Corny egg muffin

Combine 1 diced **tomato**, canned **corn kernels** and chopped **spring onion** (scallion) or fresh **chives**; add **chilli** if you like. Spoon onto toasted **English muffins**, crumble **fetta** over and grill (broil) until lightly browned. Top with a fried **egg**.

Rye bacon

Spread **rye toast** with ripe **avocado** and top with quartered **cherry tomatoes**, some cooked chopped **bacon** and grated **cheddar**.

Hawaiian

Arrange quartered **cherry tomatoes**, chopped **pineapple** and shaved **ham** on toasted **bread** and sprinkle with grated **cheddar**.

Hey pesto

Spread toasted **baguette slices** with ready-made **pesto**, and top with a sliced **semi-dried (sun-blushed) tomato** and sliced **bocconcini** (fresh baby mozzarella balls).

Chicken bagel

Spread toasted **bagels** with a little **mayonnaise**, then top with shredded leftover cooked **chicken**, canned or fresh **asparagus spears** and sliced **brie** or **camembert**.

Salmon surprise

Mix drained canned **salmon** with a spoonful of **mayonnaise** and a finely sliced **spring onion** (scallion). Spread on **toast** and top with sliced **tomato** and grated **cheddar**.

Tasty toasted sandwiches

First, pick your fillings: classic options include sliced or grated **cheese** (cheddar is great, but also try Swiss cheese, mozzarella, or soft cheeses such as brie and fetta); sliced **tomato**; **ham**, **salami**, shredded cooked **chicken** or lean fried **bacon**.

1 Preheat a frying pan over medium–low heat. Meanwhile, thinly butter two slices of bread, all the way to the edges, and place on a chopping board with the buttered sides together. On the unbuttered surface, place your fillings. Lift the top slice with the filling into the warm frying pan, buttered side down. Top with the other slice of bread, with the buttered side up.

2 Cook until the bread is golden brown and the cheese has started to melt. Flip the sandwich over to cook the other side. Be sure not to have the heat too high — you want the cheese to melt before the bread becomes too brown.

3 For a more substantial snack, serve with a fried egg on top.

Club sandwich

Preparation 10 minutes

Cooking 5 minutes

For 1

75 g (2½ oz) thin rindless
bacon (bacon strips)

3 slices rye bread

2 tablespoons mayonnaise

1 lettuce leaf

1 small tomato, sliced

¼ avocado, sliced

1 slice emmenthal or Swiss
cheese

For 2

150 g (5 oz) thin rindless
bacon (bacon strips)

6 slices rye bread

4 tablespoons mayonnaise

2 lettuce leaves

2 small tomatoes, sliced

½ avocado, sliced

2 slices emmenthal or Swiss
cheese

1 Heat a frying pan over medium–high heat.
Add the bacon and cook for 3–4 minutes, or
until crisp. Drain briefly on paper towels.

2 Meanwhile, toast the bread for each sandwich
and spread with mayonnaise.

3 Top one piece of toast with lettuce, tomato
and avocado. Add the second piece of toast and
top with a slice of cheese and the bacon.

4 Top the sandwich with the remaining slice of
toast. Secure the sandwich with a toothpick on
each side. Cut in half to serve.

Serving suggestion

Served with hot potato wedges, this classic
sandwich makes a substantial lunch or dinner.

Another idea

Add some cooked shredded chicken breast or
sliced turkey to the first sandwich layer.

*Leaving the stone in a cut
avocado will help it keep fresh
longer. Wrap the avocado in plastic
wrap and refrigerate it.*

Each serving provides
2878 kJ, 687 kcal, 39 g protein, 39 g fat (11 g saturated fat),
36 g carbohydrate (6 g sugars), 18 g fibre, 1622 mg sodium

Other ideas

- You can use beef instead of chicken.
- For a vegetarian version, sprinkle some batons of zucchini (courgette), eggplant (aubergine) and capsicum (bell pepper) with the dried spices. Fry until tender, then use instead of the chicken.

Chicken fajitas

Preparation 10 minutes

Cooking 20 minutes

For 1

1 tablespoon olive oil

1 zucchini (courgette), thinly sliced

¼ teaspoon ground cumin

¼ teaspoon ground coriander

¼ teaspoon paprika

a pinch of chilli powder

1 boneless, skinless chicken breast, about 200 g (7 oz)

2 large tortillas

1 tablespoon sour cream

½ avocado, sliced

1 small tomato, thinly sliced

1½ tablespoons grated cheddar

For 2

1½ tablespoons olive oil

2 zucchini (courgettes), thinly sliced

½ teaspoon ground cumin

½ teaspoon ground coriander

½ teaspoon paprika

a pinch of chilli powder

2 boneless, skinless chicken breasts, about 200 g (7 oz) each

4 large tortillas

2 tablespoons sour cream

1 avocado, sliced

1 large tomato, thinly sliced

¼ cup (30 g) grated cheddar

1 Heat a frying pan over medium–high heat. Add the oil and cook the zucchini for 1½ minutes on each side, or until lightly golden. Drain on paper towels.

2 Mix the dried spices together and sprinkle over both sides of the chicken. Add the chicken to the hot pan and reduce the heat to medium. Place a lid on the frying pan and cook the chicken for 6 minutes on each side. Remove from the heat and slice each breast into 6 slices.

3 Wipe the frying pan clean of oil. Add the tortillas one at a time and cook for 30 seconds on each side.

4 Lay the tortillas on a flat surface. Spread with sour cream, then top with the zucchini, avocado, tomato, chicken and cheese. Roll up and serve.

Cook's tips

- Extra tortillas can be frozen and thawed just before use.
- Avocados will keep wrapped in plastic wrap in the fridge (with the stone in) for several days.

Each serving provides
4172 kJ, 996 kcal, 58 g protein, 68 g fat (18 g saturated fat), 40 g carbohydrate (7 g sugars), 7 g fibre, 555 mg sodium

Take-away pizza is often high in fat and salt. Pizza freshly made at home is often far healthier! Using basic pantry staples and a few fresh ingredients, you can whip up a tasty pizza in no time at all.

Base

Keep a few pizza bases in the freezer (you can buy these at the supermarket). You can also use thin pita bread, or even pide (Turkish flat bread), split horizontally. Wrapped tightly in plastic wrap, these can be frozen for up to 2 months.

Sauce

Many types of tomato-based pizza and pasta sauces are now available, in jars or small tubs. Leftover sauce will keep in the fridge for up to 3 days; you can also freeze it in ice cube trays, then pop the cubes in a zip-lock bag for easy access (expel the air from the bag each time to keep it airtight).

Make your own pizza base

1 Sprinkle 2 teaspoons dry (powdered) **yeast**, 1 teaspoon **caster (superfine) sugar** and 1 teaspoon **salt** into ¾ cup (180 ml) lukewarm **water**. Stir, then stand for 5–10 minutes, until frothy.

2 Put 2 cups (300 g) **plain (all-purpose) flour** in a bowl and make a well in the centre. Add the yeast mixture and 2 tablespoons **olive oil**. Mix with a wooden spoon, then gather the dough together, turn out onto a lightly floured surface and knead for 5 minutes, until smooth.

3 Place in a clean, lightly oiled bowl; cover and stand for 45 minutes, until doubled in size. Punch down the dough, then divide into two or four portions. (At this point you can freeze any portions you don't need: wrap in plastic wrap and place in a zip-lock bag. To use, thaw the dough overnight in the fridge, then bring back to room temperature, punch down again and roll out as desired.)

4 Roll the dough out into two 22 cm (8½ inch) pizzas, or into four smaller pizzas. Place on a pizza tray or trays and top as desired.

Cheese

Mozzarella is the cheese most widely used on pizza, but you can also use cheddar where mozzarella is called for, and vice versa. You can buy pre-grated cheese, usually packaged in a zip-lock bag for convenience. It freezes well for up to 3 months, and can be used from frozen.

Toppings

These recipes serve 1, and are enough for a 20 cm (8 inch) pizza base; simply double the ingredients to serve 2. Bake in a preheated 210°C (415°F/Gas 6) oven for about 18 minutes, or until the crust is golden brown.

Prosciutto and tomato

Spread the pizza base with 1 tablespoon **tomato pizza sauce**. Top with 4 torn **basil leaves**, 2 chopped **prosciutto** slices, 3 thickly sliced **cherry tomatoes** and 1 sliced **bocconcini** (fresh baby mozzarella ball). Serve scattered with small fresh basil leaves.

Satay chicken

Spread the pizza base with 1 tablespoon **satay sauce** and sprinkle with 2 tablespoons grated **cheddar**. Top with ½ cup (90 g) shredded cooked **chicken**, 1 sliced **spring onion (scallion)** and another 2 tablespoons grated cheddar. Serve with a dollop of **natural (plain) yogurt**, with a few **snow pea (mangetout) sprouts** scattered over the top.

Asparagus and salmon

Spread the pizza base with 1 tablespoon **cream cheese**. Top with 3 **asparagus spears**, thinly sliced diagonally, and ½ teaspoon **capers**. Serve topped with 25 g (1 oz) **smoked salmon** slices, a drizzle of **olive oil** and **lemon wedges**.

Pumpkin and pesto

Spread the pizza base with 1 tablespoon ready-made **pesto**. Top with 90 g (3 oz) cooked diced **pumpkin** (winter squash), 25 g (1 oz) crumbled **blue cheese** and 1½ tablespoons **walnut pieces**. Serve with **rocket** (arugula) leaves scattered over the top.

Rosemary and garlic potato

In a bowl, combine 1 tablespoon **olive oil**, ½ small crushed **garlic** clove and ½ teaspoon chopped **fresh rosemary**; season with **salt** and freshly ground **black pepper**. Brush half the mixture over the pizza base. Arrange 1 small thinly sliced desiree **potato** on top, overlapping slightly, and brush with the remaining mixture.

Gourmet vegetarian

Spread the pizza base with 1 tablespoon **tomato pizza sauce**. Top with ½ small thinly sliced **red onion**, ½ small sliced **red capsicum** (bell pepper), 2 quartered **artichoke hearts** and 30 g (1 oz) sliced **button mushrooms**. Crumble 50 g (1¾ oz) **fetta** over the top.

Spicy salami

Spread the pizza base with 1 tablespoon **tomato pizza sauce**. Top with 50 g (1¾ oz) shredded **salami**, 40 g (1½ oz) sliced **roasted red capsicum** (bell pepper), 5 halved **cherry tomatoes** and 10 g (¼ oz) shredded **baby English spinach**. Sprinkle with 2 tablespoons grated **mozzarella**.

Brown fried rice

Preparation 10 minutes

Cooking 10 minutes

For 1

1 egg, beaten

1 teaspoon salt-reduced soy sauce

1 tablespoon peanut oil

1½ slices rindless bacon (bacon strips), diced

50 g (1¾ oz) peeled raw prawns (uncooked shrimp)

3 baby corn, halved lengthwise

6 snow peas (mangetout), thinly sliced lengthwise

1 cup (185 g) cooked brown rice

1 teaspoon kecap manis

1 teaspoon oyster sauce

1 spring onion (scallion), sliced

For 2

2 eggs, beaten

2 teaspoons salt-reduced soy sauce

1 tablespoon peanut oil

3 slices rindless bacon (bacon strips), diced

100 g (3½ oz) peeled raw prawns (uncooked shrimp)

6 baby corn, halved lengthwise

12 snow peas (mangetout), thinly sliced lengthwise

2 cups (370 g) cooked brown rice

2 teaspoons kecap manis

2 teaspoons oyster sauce

2 spring onions (scallions), sliced

1 Whisk the eggs and soy sauce together in a bowl. Heat the oil in a hot wok over medium–high heat. Pour in the egg mixture and swirl it around the pan to form an omelette; cook for 1 minute, or until just set. Slide the omelette onto a clean board, roll it up and thinly slice.

2 Add the bacon to the hot wok and cook for 2–3 minutes, or until crisp. Add the prawns and cook for a further 2 minutes, or until they turn pink and curl up.

3 Add the corn and cook for 1 minute, then add the snow peas and cook for a further minute. Stir in the rice, kecap manis and oyster sauce until well combined and allow to heat through.

4 Stir in the spring onion and serve.

Cook's tip

Use frozen mixed stir-fry vegetables instead of fresh vegetables, or frozen peas and corn.

Each serving provides
2852 kJ, 681 kcal, 39 g protein, 23 g fat (6 g saturated fat), 79 g carbohydrate (17 g sugars), 4 g fibre, 1942 mg sodium

Here's a perfect way to use up leftover cooked brown rice or white rice. You can use a diced boneless, skinless chicken thigh instead of prawns.

High in protein, fibre, vitamins
and minerals, quinoa (pronounced 'keen-wah')
is a highly nutritious grain-like seed, with
a mild flavour. Here's a great recipe
if you've never tried it before.

Creamy mushroom quinoa

Preparation 10 minutes

Cooking 25 minutes

One-pot

For 1

1 tablespoon butter

1 tablespoon olive oil

½ onion, finely chopped

200 g (7 oz) sliced mushrooms

1 small zucchini (courgette), halved lengthwise, thickly sliced

1 small clove garlic, finely chopped

2 sprigs fresh thyme

½ tablespoon chopped fresh sage

¼ cup (50 g) quinoa

½ cup (125 ml) chicken stock

2 tablespoons pouring cream

1 tablespoon grated parmesan

For 2

1½ tablespoons butter

1 tablespoon olive oil

1 small onion, finely chopped

400 g (14 oz) sliced mushrooms

1 large zucchini (courgette), halved lengthwise, thickly sliced

1 large clove garlic, finely chopped

3–4 sprigs fresh thyme

1 tablespoon chopped fresh sage

½ cup (100 g) quinoa

1 cup (250 ml) chicken stock

⅓ cup (80 ml) pouring cream

2 tablespoons grated parmesan

1 Heat the butter and oil in a large saucepan over medium heat. Add the onion and cook for 1 minute. Add the mushrooms, zucchini, garlic, thyme and sage and cook for 5 minutes, stirring occasionally.

2 Stir in the quinoa and stock, then cover and simmer for 15 minutes.

3 Stir in the cream and parmesan. Cover and simmer for a further 5 minutes. Serve hot.

Each serving provides
3096 kJ, 739 kcal, 20 g protein, 54 g fat (24 g saturated fat), 44 g carbohydrate (6 g sugars), 10 g fibre, 575 mg sodium

Leftover magic

- Use any leftover cream in our **Pork with creamy garlic mustard sauce** (page 168).
- Leftover chicken stock can be frozen in ice cube trays and used as required.

Cook's tips

- Button, shiitake, oyster and Swiss brown mushrooms are all delicious in this dish.
- Stock (bouillon) cubes and stock powder are handy for making up smaller amounts of stock.

Quesadillas

Preparation 10 minutes

Cooking 5 minutes (for 1), 10 minutes (for 2)

For 1

2 flour tortillas

2 tablespoons refried beans

¼ cup (45 g) shredded cooked chicken

¼ cup (30 g) grated cheddar

1 spring onion (scallion), chopped

1 tablespoon roughly chopped coriander (cilantro)

oil, for pan-frying

1 tablespoon sour cream

1 tablespoon bottled salsa

For 2

4 flour tortillas

⅓ cup (80 g) refried beans

½ (90 g) shredded cooked chicken

½ cup (60 g) grated cheddar

2 spring onions (scallions), chopped

2 tablespoons roughly chopped coriander (cilantro)

oil, for pan-frying

2 tablespoons sour cream

2 tablespoons bottled salsa

Each serving provides
1892 kJ, 451 kcal, 24 g protein, 29 g fat (12 g saturated fat),
24 g carbohydrate (4 g sugars), 5 g fibre, 579 mg sodium

1 Place half the tortillas on a plate. Spread with the refried beans, then top with the chicken, cheese, spring onion and coriander. Top with the remaining tortilla or tortillas.

2 Heat a non-stick frying pan over medium heat and lightly oil it. Carefully slide a quesadilla into the pan and cook for 1–2 minutes, or until lightly golden underneath.

3 Turn the quesadilla over, cook for 1–2 minutes, then transfer to a cutting board. If making two quesadillas, cook the other one in the same way.

4 Cut into wedges and serve with the sour cream and salsa.

Other ideas

- Use cream cheese instead of refried beans; top with shredded ham, spring onion, coriander and grated cheese.
- Fill the quesadilla with mashed cooked sweet potato, canned corn kernels and grated cheese.

Cook's tips

- You can use a sandwich press to toast the quesadillas.
- Use the remaining refried beans in a taco beans or beef mixture. The sour cream and bottled salsa will keep well in the fridge.

Cook's tips

Warming the tortilla makes it
easier to press into a basket shape
without tearing it.

Instead of serving the filling in a
tortilla basket, simply wrap it up in
the warmed flat tortilla.

Bean tortilla basket

Preparation 10 minutes

Cooking 10 minutes

For 1

1 flour tortilla

olive oil spray

125 g (4 oz) can red kidney beans, drained

¼ avocado, diced

¼ tomato, diced

1 tablespoon chopped roasted red capsicum (bell pepper)

1 tablespoon coriander (cilantro) leaves

1 small spring onion (scallion), chopped

1 tablespoon lime juice

1 tablespoon grated cheddar

For 2

2 flour tortillas

olive oil spray

2 x 125 g (4 oz) cans red kidney beans, drained

½ avocado, diced

½ tomato, diced

2 tablespoons chopped roasted red capsicum (bell pepper)

2 tablespoons coriander (cilantro) leaves

1 spring onion (scallion), chopped

2 tablespoons lime juice

2 tablespoons grated cheddar

1 Preheat the oven to 180°C (350°F/Gas 4). Warm each tortilla in a microwave for 20 seconds to soften it. Press each tortilla into a 1 cup (250 ml) ramekin to create a basket shape. Spray with olive oil spray and bake for 8–10 minutes, or until lightly golden. Allow to cool.

2 Combine the beans, avocado, tomato, capsicum, coriander, spring onion and lime juice in a bowl. Season with salt and freshly ground black pepper and gently stir until combined.

3 Spoon the bean salad into each tortilla basket. Sprinkle with the cheese and serve.

Leftover magic

- Bottled roasted red capsicum keeps for about a week in the fridge after opening.

- Instead of using half or quarter of a tomato, use some halved cherry tomatoes.

Each serving provides
1408 kJ, 336 kcal, 11 g protein, 21 g fat (5 g saturated fat), 25 g carbohydrate (4 g sugars), 7 g fibre, 478 mg sodium

Colcannon

Preparation 10 minutes

Cooking 20 minutes

For 1

1 large (175 g/6 oz) mashing
   potato

2 tablespoons milk

1 tablespoon butter, cubed

½ cup (40 g) shredded savoy
   cabbage

1 spring onion (scallion),
   chopped

For 2

2 large (350 g/12 oz) mashing
   potatoes

⅓ cup (80 ml) milk

2 tablespoons butter, cubed

1 cup (75 g) shredded savoy
   cabbage

2 spring onions (scallions),
   chopped

1 Peel each potato and cut into 4 cm (1½ inch) chunks. Place in a large saucepan of cold water, cover and bring to a boil. Cook, uncovered, for 12–15 minutes, or until the potato is tender but not falling apart. Drain well, then return to the saucepan and mash roughly with a potato masher.

2 Add the milk and half the butter and beat with a wooden spoon until fluffy. Keep warm.

3 Melt the remaining butter in a small non-stick frying pan over medium–high heat. Add the cabbage and spring onion and cook, stirring, for 1–2 minutes, or until the cabbage has softened.

4 Stir the mixture through the mashed potato and season with salt and freshly ground black pepper. Serve immediately.

Each serving provides
1215 kJ, 290 kcal, 6 g protein, 17 g fat (11 g saturated fat), 26 g carbohydrate (4 g sugars), 4 g fibre, 167 mg sodium

Serving suggestion

This traditional Irish potato and cabbage mash is delicious as a side dish to a light meal, or alongside stews, casseroles and pan-fried meats.

Cook's tip

Excellent mashing potatoes include spunta, sebago, pontiac and coliban.

Other ideas

- Replace the milk with cream.
- Fry some chopped bacon in the frying pan until golden before adding the cabbage and spring onion.
- Replace the cabbage with kale, spinach or silverbeet (Swiss chard).
- Mix in some chopped fresh parsley just before serving.

Quick ideas for... baked jacket potatoes

A baked jacket potato with a tasty filling or topping makes a wholesome, low-fuss light meal, or an easy side dish. Plan ahead a little, so you can cook another dish in the oven at the same time.

Choose your potato

Use a type of potato suitable for baking. You will want a floury or all-purpose variety, rather than one that is labelled a 'waxy' or 'boiling' potato. Great baking potatoes include sebago, coliban, russet burbank and desiree. You can use sweet potatoes, too.

Bake the potato

Preheat the oven to 200°C (400°F/Gas 6). Scrub one or two 300 g (10 oz) potatoes under running water with a stiff brush to remove all the dirt. Pat dry with paper towels, and prick several times with a fork or small sharp knife. (If you don't prick the skin, the internal pressure can build up during cooking, and the potato can burst, making a mess of your oven!) Bake for 1½ hours, or until the skin is crisp and the flesh inside is soft when tested with a skewer or small knife.

Super-speedy shortcut

Rub the scrubbed, dried and pricked potato or potatoes with a little olive oil, then place on a sheet of paper towel. Microwave on high for 8 minutes, turning over halfway through cooking. The 'jacket' will not become as crisp as when baked in a conventional oven, but it certainly cuts the cooking time!

Top or fill

Cut a slice from the top of the baked potato (a flat side), and scoop out the cooked flesh, leaving a shell roughly 1 cm (½ inch) thick. Roughly mash the scooped-out flesh with your filling ingredients, season to taste with salt and freshly ground black pepper, then spoon back into the shell.

Alternatively, cut the potato in half horizontally, use a fork to 'rough up' the cut surface, then spoon or sprinkle your topping over.

Either way, you can then reheat the potatoes in the oven for 10–15 minutes, especially if you need to melt any cheese in the filling or topping.

Easy cheesy

Mash the flesh with grated **cheddar**, sliced **spring onion (scallion)** or chopped fresh **chives** and a little **butter**. Try different cheeses, such as a creamy brie, piquant blue or crumbly fetta.

Happy herbs

Mash the flesh with chopped **fresh herbs** such as rosemary, chives, parsley, thyme or basil. Use just one herb, or a combination. Add a little **butter** and season with **salt** and freshly ground **black pepper**. (A little chopped fresh **chilli** and/or **garlic**, sautéed first in oil or butter, will add a huge flavour hit.)

Snappy salsa

Scoop out the potato and mash with grated **cheddar**. Return to the shell and top with a simple salsa made from chopped **tomato**, drained canned **corn kernels** and diced **avocado**, with a squeeze of lemon or lime juice.

Savoury seafood

Mix the mashed flesh with a small drained can of **salmon**, **tuna** or **sardines** — or use small cooked peeled **prawns** (shrimp), sliced **smoked salmon**, flaked poached **cod**, **kippers** or **haddock**. Make it special with a dollop of **sour cream**.

Vegetable power

Sauté sliced **zucchini** (courgette), sliced **button mushrooms**, **onion** and **garlic** in a little **olive oil**. Add some halved **cherry tomatoes** and sauté until soft. Season to taste and serve over the potato.

Meat lover's

Mix the mashed flesh with **salami**; or **mustard** and chopped **ham**; **roast beef** and **horseradish cream**; or fried chopped **bacon** or **chorizo**.

Mediterranean magic

Halve the baked potato and serve topped with the **bolognese** mixture on page 160, or the **ratatouille** mixture on page 110. Top with grated **parmesan** and chopped **basil**.

Elegant egg

Mix the mashed flesh with chopped **hard-boiled eggs**, snipped fresh **chives** and a spoonful of **mayonnaise**, then scoop back into the shells.

Side show

If you are serving the potato as a side dish, you may want to simply add a knob of butter to melt through the hot flesh — or a dollop of sour cream, mayonnaise, crème fraîche, cream cheese or natural (plain) yogurt. A drizzle of sweet chilli sauce is also great.

Here's a perfect use for leftover cooked macaroni or pasta, which will also reduce the recipe's cooking time.

Cheesy tuna mornay pots

Preparation 10 minutes

Cooking 30 minutes

For 1

¼ cup (40 g) macaroni pasta

3 teaspoons butter

1 spring onion (scallion), chopped

1 tablespoon plain (all-purpose) flour

½ cup (125 ml) milk

95 g (3 oz) can tuna in brine, drained

125 g (4 oz) can corn kernels, drained

2 tablespoons grated cheddar

2 teaspoons dry breadcrumbs

pinch of paprika

For 2

½ cup (80 g) macaroni pasta

1½ tablespoons butter

2 spring onions (scallions), chopped

2 tablespoons plain (all-purpose) flour

1 cup (250 ml) milk

185 g (6 oz) can tuna in brine, drained

2 x 125 g (4 oz) cans corn kernels, drained

⅓ cup (40 g) grated cheddar

1 tablespoon dry breadcrumbs

pinch of paprika

1 Preheat the oven to 180°C (350°F/Gas 4). Lightly grease a 1 cup (250 ml) ramekin for each serving. Bring a saucepan of water to a boil and add the pasta. Cover and bring back to a boil, then cook, uncovered, for 10 minutes, or until the pasta is al dente. Drain.

2 Meanwhile, melt the butter in a medium saucepan over medium heat. Add the spring onion and cook, stirring, for 1 minute, or until softened. Add the flour and stir for 1 minute. Remove from the heat and gradually whisk in the milk until smooth. Return to the heat and cook, stirring, until the mixture boils and thickens.

3 Remove the sauce from the heat. Stir in the pasta, tuna, corn and half the cheese. Season with salt and freshly ground black pepper, then spoon into each ramekin. Combine the remaining cheese, breadcrumbs and paprika and sprinkle over the top.

4 Bake for 15–18 minutes, or until the topping is golden brown. Serve hot.

Each serving provides
2686 kJ, 641 kcal, 37 g protein, 27 g fat (16 g saturated fat), 62 g carbohydrate (10 g sugars), 5 g fibre, 624 mg sodium

Salmon fish cake

Preparation 15 minutes

- -

Cooking 20 minutes

For 1

1 desiree potato, about 180 g (6 oz), peeled

105 g (3½ oz) can red salmon, drained, skin and bones removed

¼ teaspoon grated lemon zest

½ teaspoon chopped fresh dill

1 teaspoon chopped fresh parsley

2 tablespoons plain (all-purpose) flour

1 egg, lightly whisked

¼ cup (25 g) dry breadcrumbs

vegetable oil, for pan-frying

½ cup (20 g) baby rocket (arugula) leaves

Caper mayonnaise

1½ tablespoons whole-egg mayonnaise

½ teaspoon chopped capers

1 teaspoon lemon juice

For 2

2 desiree potatoes, about 360 g (12¾ oz), peeled

210 g (7½ oz) can red salmon, drained, skin and bones removed

½ teaspoon grated lemon zest

1 teaspoon chopped fresh dill

2 teaspoons chopped fresh parsley

⅓ cup (50 g) plain (all-purpose) flour

2 eggs, lightly whisked

½ cup (50 g) dry breadcrumbs

vegetable oil, for pan-frying

1 cup (40 g) baby rocket (arugula) leaves

Caper mayonnaise

3 tablespoons whole-egg mayonnaise

1 teaspoon chopped capers

2 teaspoons lemon juice

Each serving provides
3077 kJ, 735 kcal, 36 g protein, 39 g fat (7 g saturated fat), 59 g carbohydrate (3 g sugars), 5 g fibre, 761 mg sodium

Leftover magic

When boiling potatoes, plan ahead and boil a few extra to use in this recipe. It will make the salmon cakes much quicker to prepare.

1 Cut the potatoes into 3 cm (1¼ inch) chunks and place in a saucepan of cold water. Cover, bring to a boil and cook, uncovered, for 10–12 minutes, or until tender but not falling apart. Drain well, then return to the pan and roughly mash with a potato masher.

2 Combine the potato, salmon, lemon zest, dill and parsley. Season with sea salt and freshly ground black pepper, then shape into one 8 cm (3¼ inch) patty per person.

3 Place the flour, egg and breadcrumbs in separate bowls. Coat the patty or patties in the flour, shaking off any excess. Coat in the egg, then the breadcrumbs.

4 Heat a small frying pan over medium heat. Pour in 1.5 cm (⅝ inch) of oil. When the oil is hot, cook the patty or patties for 2–3 minutes on each side, or until golden. Drain on paper towels.

5 Combine the caper mayonnaise ingredients and season to taste. Serve with the fish patties and rocket.

Fresh rice paper rolls

Preparation 15 minutes

- -

Cooking None

Quick

No-Cook

For 1

15 g (½ oz) rice vermicelli noodles

¼ red capsicum (bell pepper)

¼ carrot

½ Lebanese or other small
   cucumber, seeds removed

3 snow peas (mangetout)

1 spring onion (scallion)

3 round rice paper wrappers

3 fresh mint or basil leaves

3 coriander (cilantro) leaves

Dipping sauce

2 teaspoons hoisin sauce

1 teaspoon salt-reduced soy sauce

drop of sesame oil

a pinch of crushed nuts

For 2

30 g (1 oz) rice vermicelli noodles

½ red capsicum (bell pepper)

½ carrot

1 Lebanese or other small
   cucumber, seeds removed

6 snow peas (mangetout)

2 spring onions (scallions)

6 round rice paper wrappers

6 fresh mint or basil leaves

6 coriander (cilantro) leaves

Dipping sauce

1 tablespoon hoisin sauce

2 teaspoons salt-reduced soy
   sauce

drop of sesame oil

a pinch of crushed nuts

Leftover magic

- Use any leftover noodles in soups and salads.
- Use any remaining herbs and vegetables in salads or stir-fries.

Cook's tip

Don't leave the rolls sitting exposed to the air for too long or the wrappers will dry out. Cover them with plastic wrap or a clean damp cloth.

Other ideas

- Include 1 cooked king prawn (shrimp) in each spring roll. Peel and devein the prawns, then cut them in half crosswise.
- Add strips of barbecued duck or roast pork.

- -

Each serving provides
1064 kJ, 254 kcal, 5 g protein, 3 g fat (<1 g saturated fat), 52 g carbohydrate (9 g sugars), 4 g fibre, 401 mg sodium

1 Place the noodles in a heatproof bowl. Cover with boiling water and stand for 6–8 minutes, or until softened. Drain and cut into shorter lengths using scissors.

2 Meanwhile, thinly slice the vegetables. Mix the dipping sauce ingredients in a small bowl.

3 Working with one sheet at a time, place a rice paper wrapper in a bowl of warm water for about 30 seconds, or until softened. Place on a clean board and pat dry with a paper towel.

4 If making 3 rolls, place one-third of the noodles, vegetables and herbs in the centre; if making 6 rolls, place one-sixth in the centre. Fold one side of the rice paper over to partially cover the filling, then fold in the two sides. Continue rolling into a cigar shape, enclosing the filling.

5 Repeat with the remaining wrappers and filling ingredients. Serve with the dipping sauce.

HEF'S SALAD Prosciutto, pear and parmesan salad Fat

Duck salad ASIAN RICE SALAD Duck salad BEETR

Gado gado Fattoush salad Panzanella salad with chic

Step-by-step

UICK IDEAS FOR... SALAD LEAVES Couscous and c

Beetroot and fetta salad Gado gado Step-by-step Asian

and noodle salad POTATO, EGG AND BACON SALAD Ch

Quick ideas for... side salads Fresh tuna and green bea

salads

Fresh tuna and green bean salad

Preparation 10 minutes

Cooking 7 minutes

For 1

140 g (4½ oz) tuna steak

1½ tablespoons olive oil

50 g (1¾ oz) green beans,
trimmed

2 teaspoons red wine vinegar

½ teaspoon dijon mustard

a pinch of caster (superfine)
sugar

50 g (1¾ oz) baby cos (romaine)
lettuce leaves

6 red or yellow cherry tomatoes,
halved

6 pitted kalamata olives

For 2

2 x 140 g (4½ oz) tuna steaks

2½ tablespoons olive oil

100 g (3½ oz) green beans,
trimmed

1 tablespoon red wine vinegar

1 teaspoon dijon mustard

a pinch of caster (superfine)
sugar

100 g (3½ oz) baby cos (romaine)
lettuce leaves

12 red or yellow cherry tomatoes,
halved

12 pitted kalamata olives

1 Season the tuna on both sides with salt and freshly ground black pepper. Heat 2 teaspoons of the oil in a small non-stick frying pan over medium–high heat. Add the tuna and cook for 2–3 minutes on each side for medium–rare, or until cooked to your liking. Remove from the pan and leave to cool. Flake the flesh into chunks.

2 Meanwhile, bring a small saucepan of water to a boil. Add the beans and cook for 2 minutes, or until just tender but still crisp. Drain and refresh under cold running water.

3 Whisk together the remaining oil with the vinegar, mustard and sugar.

4 Arrange the lettuce leaves on a plate or plates. Gently toss together the beans, tomatoes, olives, tuna and dressing in a bowl. Arrange over the lettuce and serve immediately.

Other ideas

- Replace the tuna with pan-fried salmon or prawns (shrimp).
- Use canned tuna instead of fresh fish.
- Toss the salad through cooked pasta.

Each serving provides
2281 kJ, 545 kcal, 38 g protein, 39 g fat (7 g saturated fat),
8 g carbohydrate (4 g sugars), 4 g fibre, 441 mg sodium

Chef's salad

Preparation 10 minutes

Cooking 10 minutes

Quick

For 1

1 egg

50 g (1¾ oz) baby cos (romaine)
　　lettuce leaves

5 grape tomatoes

½ small Lebanese or other small
　　cucumber, chopped

1 slice ham off the bone, about
　　60 g (2 oz), cut into thick strips

1 slice jarlsberg cheese, cut into
　　thick strips

1 tablespoon mayonnaise

1 teaspoon lemon juice

½ teaspoon dijon mustard

½ teaspoon honey

For 2

2 eggs

100 g (3½ oz) baby cos (romaine)
　　lettuce leaves

10 grape tomatoes

1 small Lebanese or other small
　　cucumber, chopped

2 slices ham off the bone, about
　　125 g (4 oz), cut into thick strips

2 slices jarlsberg cheese, cut into
　　thick strips

2 tablespoons mayonnaise

2 teaspoons lemon juice

1 teaspoon dijon mustard

1 teaspoon honey

1 Place the egg or eggs in a small saucepan of cold water and bring to a boil over high heat. Reduce the heat to medium and gently boil, uncovered, for 7 minutes, stirring occasionally. Drain and cool under cold running water. Leave to cool, then peel and cut into quarters.

2 Place the lettuce leaves on a plate or plates and arrange the tomatoes, cucumber, egg, ham and cheese over the top.

3 Combine the mayonnaise, lemon juice, mustard and honey in a bowl. Season with salt and freshly ground black pepper and mix until well combined. Drizzle over the salad and serve immediately.

Another idea

Replace the mayonnaise dressing with a ready-made French dressing.

Each serving provides
1293 kJ, 309 kcal, 24 g protein, 19 g fat (6 g saturated fat), 11 g carbohydrate (10 g sugars), 3 g fibre, 1265 mg sodium

Panzanella salad with chicken

Preparation 10 minutes

Cooking 15 minutes

For 1

- 1 thick slice day-old sourdough bread, about 55 g (2 oz)
- 2 tablespoons olive oil
- 2 chicken tenderloins (tenders)
- 1/4 roasted red capsicum (bell pepper), chopped
- 8 cherry tomatoes, halved
- 6 pitted kalamata olives
- 12 small basil leaves, torn
- 2 1/2 teaspoons red wine vinegar

For 2

- 2 thick slices day-old sourdough bread, about 110 g (3 1/2 oz)
- 3 tablespoons olive oil
- 4 chicken tenderloins (tenders)
- 1/2 roasted red capsicum (bell pepper), chopped
- 16 cherry tomatoes, halved
- 12 pitted kalamata olives
- 24 small basil leaves, torn
- 1 1/2 tablespoons red wine vinegar

1 Cut the bread into 2.5 cm (1 inch) cubes. Heat 3 teaspoons of the oil in a small non-stick frying pan over medium heat. Add the bread cubes and fry for 4–5 minutes, turning often, until crisp and golden brown all over. Wipe the pan clean with paper towel.

2 Heat another teaspoon of the oil in the pan over medium–high heat. Season the chicken with salt and freshly ground black pepper, then cook for 4 minutes on each side, or until cooked through. Cut cooked chicken in half.

3 Combine the capsicum, tomatoes, olives, basil and bread in a bowl. Whisk together the remaining oil and vinegar and season with salt and pepper. Add the dressing to the salad and toss until well combined. Add the chicken and toss lightly.

4 Spoon the chicken and salad onto a plate or plates and serve immediately.

Cook's tip

Buy roasted capsicums in jars or from the delicatessen section of supermarkets.

Each serving provides
3147 kJ, 751 kcal, 47 g protein, 53 g fat (9 g saturated fat), 22 g carbohydrate (4 g sugars), 3 g fibre, 618 mg sodium

Fattoush salad

Preparation 10 minutes

Cooking 10 minutes

Quick

For 1

½ pita bread

1½ tablespoons olive oil

½ teaspoon sumac

½ Lebanese or other small
cucumber, chopped

½ tomato, chopped

¼ small red onion, chopped

2 tablespoons chopped fresh parsley

3 fresh mint leaves, chopped

½ small clove garlic, crushed

1 tablespoon lemon juice

40 g (1½ oz) fetta

For 2

1 pita bread

3 tablespoons olive oil

1 teaspoon sumac

1 small Lebanese or other small
cucumber, chopped

1 tomato, chopped

½ small red onion, chopped

4 tablespoons chopped fresh parsley

6 fresh mint leaves, chopped

1 small clove garlic, crushed

2 tablespoons lemon juice

80 g (2¾ oz) fetta

1 Preheat the oven to 180°C (350°F/Gas 4). Line a baking tray with baking (parchment) paper.

2 Split the pita bread in half and generously brush both sides with some of the oil. Sprinkle with the sumac and bake for 6–8 minutes, or until the bread is crisp and golden. Allow to cool, then break into pieces.

3 In a bowl, combine the cucumber, tomato, onion, parsley, mint and pita bread pieces.

4 Whisk together the garlic, lemon juice and remaining olive oil. Season with salt and freshly ground black pepper. Pour over the salad and gently toss together.

5 Crumble the fetta over and serve immediately.

Other ideas

■ Replace the lemon juice with red wine vinegar.

■ Add some radish slices for extra bite.

■ Instead of the fetta, top the salad with a slice of fried haloumi cheese.

Cook's tip

Sumac gives a tangy, lemony flavour to meats and salad. You'll find it in the spice section of most supermarkets and good delicatessens.

Each serving provides
2027 kJ, 484 kcal, 12 g protein, 37 g fat (10 g saturated fat), 25 g carbohydrate (4 g sugars), 3 g fibre, 650 mg sodium

Salads add a rainbow of colour to a plate, as well as a huge array of health-giving nutrients. Try these salads with meat, fish or chicken dishes. These recipes serve 1; simply double the recipes to serve 2.

All-time favourites

These three salads do require a bit of cooking — but if you cook up some extra potato, pasta or rice from a previous meal, you can hold some over for mixing up these much-loved salads.

Potato salad

Cut 3 small **new potatoes** in half and place in a small saucepan. Cover with cold **water**, cover the pan and bring to a boil. Tilt the lid so it partially covers the pan, then cook for 10 minutes, or until the potatoes are tender. Drain and cool. Mix 1 tablespoon **mayonnaise** and 1 tablespoon **sour cream** until well combined; stir in 1 sliced **spring onion** (scallion) and season with salt and freshly ground black pepper. If you like, add a little **wholegrain mustard** or finely chopped **gherkin** (pickle) to the dressing. Gently mix through the potatoes and serve at room temperature.

Pasta salad

Cook ½ cup (about 90 g) **penne or spiral pasta** in a saucepan of boiling water for 10 minutes, or until al dente. (If using leftovers, you'll need about 1 cup cooked pasta.) Rinse under cold running water and drain well. Place in a bowl with 4 chopped **cherry tomatoes**, 1 tablespoon chopped pitted **olives**, 2 tablespoons chopped **semi-dried (sun-blushed) tomatoes** and about 1 tablespoon chopped fresh **basil**. Gently toss with 1 tablespoon **olive oil** and 2 teaspoons **white wine vinegar**. Serve at room temperature.

Rice salad

Cook ¼ cup (50 g) **long-grain white rice** in a saucepan of boiling water for 10 minutes, or until just tender. (If you are using leftovers, you'll need about ¾ cup/140 g cooked rice.) In the last 2 minutes of cooking, add 2 tablespoons frozen **corn kernels**. Drain well and place in a bowl. Stir in 2–3 teaspoons **lemon juice**, to taste, and 2 teaspoons **olive oil.** Add 2 teaspoons chopped fresh **parsley**, ¼ finely diced Lebanese or other small **cucumber**, and ¼ finely diced small **red capsicum** (bell pepper). Season with salt and freshly ground black pepper and toss together.

Cool classics

Tomato salsa

In a bowl, combine 1 seeded and diced **tomato**, ½ finely chopped **spring onion** (scallion), 1 tablespoon chopped fresh **coriander** (cilantro), 1 teaspoon chopped fresh **mint**, 1 tablespoon **lime juice** and a pinch each of **ground coriander** and **cumin**. (If you are doubling the recipe, keep the lime juice measurement the same.) Stand for 30 minutes to allow the flavours to develop. Just before serving, season to taste with salt and freshly ground black pepper.

Tabbouleh

Place 2 tablespoons **burghul** (bulgur) in a bowl and pour in enough boiling water to cover. Leave to soak for 15 minutes, then drain. Place in a clean tea towel (dish towel), wrap tightly and squeeze out the excess water. Place the burghul in a bowl with ½ seeded and finely chopped **tomato**, ¼ finely diced Lebanese or other small **cucumber**, 2 teaspoons finely chopped fresh **mint**, 2 tablespoons finely chopped fresh **parsley**, ½ finely chopped **spring onion** (scallion), 2 teaspoons **olive oil** and 1 tablespoon **lemon juice**. Mix together well, season with **salt** and freshly ground **black pepper** and serve.

Salads are wonderfully versatile, so don't be afraid to experiment with other ingredients you have on hand.

Coleslaw

Place ¼ cup (15 g) each shredded **white cabbage** and shredded **red cabbage** — or ½ cup (30 g) of just one type — in a bowl. Add 2 tablespoons roughly grated **carrot** and 1 finely chopped **spring onion** (scallion). Whisk together 1 tablespoon **mayonnaise** and 1 teaspoon **lemon juice**, drizzle over the salad and toss to combine. Season to taste with salt and freshly ground black pepper. Serve immediately, or cover and refrigerate until required.

Cucumber salad

Cut 1 Lebanese or other small **cucumber** in half lengthwise, then remove the seeds using a teaspoon. Slice the flesh diagonally and place in a bowl. Mix together 1 tablespoon thick (Greek-style) **yogurt**, 1 teaspoon **olive oil**, 1 teaspoon **lemon juice**, 1 teaspoon chopped **fresh dill** and ½ sliced **spring onion** (scallion), then season with salt and freshly ground black pepper. Add to the cucumber slices and gently mix until well combined. Serve immediately, or cover and refrigerate until required.

Carrot salad

Toast 1 tablespoon **pine nuts** in a small non-stick frying pan over medium heat, without any oil, for 3 minutes, or until just golden. Add 2 teaspoons **currants** and 1 tablespoon **orange juice** and stir to combine. Tip the mixture into a bowl and add 1 grated **carrot**, 2 teaspoons chopped **fresh parsley** and 2 teaspoons **olive oil**. Season to taste with **salt** and freshly ground **black pepper** and mix well. Serve immediately, or cover and refrigerate until required.

Beetroot and fetta salad

Preparation 10 minutes

- -

Cooking None

For 1

3 canned baby beetroot (beets),
    about 100 g (3½ oz)
½ cup (25 g) baby English
    spinach leaves
¼ cup (35 g) crumbled fetta
1½ tablespoons walnut pieces
1½ teaspoons olive oil
1 teaspoon red wine vinegar
½ teaspoon snipped fresh chives

For 2

6 canned baby beetroot (beets),
    about 200 g (7 oz)
1 cup (50 g) baby English
    spinach leaves
½ cup (75 g) crumbled fetta
3 tablespoons walnut pieces
3 teaspoons olive oil
2 teaspoons red wine vinegar
1 teaspoon snipped fresh chives

1 Drain the beetroot on paper towels and cut them into wedges. Gently toss the beetroot and spinach leaves together in a bowl.

2 Scatter the fetta and walnuts over the top.

3 Whisk together the olive oil, vinegar and chives and season with salt and freshly ground black pepper. Drizzle over the salad and serve.

Serving suggestion

This salad is delicious with barbecued meats and crusty bread.

Other ideas

- Replace the beetroot with cooked warm broad (fava) beans.
- Use marinated fetta, and use the oil from the fetta in the dressing.

- -

Each serving provides
1271 kJ, 303 kcal, 10 g protein, 25 g fat (7 g saturated fat),
10 g carbohydrate (10 g sugars), 4 g fibre, 704 mg sodium

Cook's tips

There is no need to peel small new potatoes as their skins are very thin. Leaving the skin on helps retain their flavour during cooking and increases their healthy fibre content. You can also use leftover cooked potatoes or boiled eggs in the salad. Add some baby spinach leaves for a complete meal.

Other ideas

- Instead of using both sour cream and mayonnaise, just use one or the other.
- Replace the white wine vinegar with lemon juice, and the spring onion with snipped fresh chives.
- Use prosciutto or salami instead of bacon.

Potato, egg and bacon salad

Preparation 10 minutes

Cooking 20 minutes

For 1

- 3–4 small new potatoes (150 g/5 oz), cut in half
- 1 egg
- ½ teaspoon olive oil
- 1 small slice rindless bacon (bacon strip), chopped
- 2 teaspoons sour cream
- 1 tablespoon good-quality mayonnaise
- ¼ teaspoon dijon mustard
- ½ teaspoon white wine vinegar
- 1 small spring onion (scallion), sliced

For 2

- 6–8 small new potatoes (300 g/10 oz), cut in half
- 2 eggs
- 1 teaspoon olive oil
- 2 small slices rindless bacon (bacon strips), chopped
- 1 tablespoon sour cream
- 2 tablespoons good-quality mayonnaise
- ½ teaspoon dijon mustard
- 1 teaspoon white wine vinegar
- 1 spring onion (scallion), sliced

1 Put the potatoes in a saucepan, cover with cold water and bring to a boil. Cook for 10–15 minutes, or until tender. Drain well.

2 Meanwhile, place the egg or eggs in a small saucepan and cover with cold water. Bring to a boil and cook for 10 minutes, timing from when the water starts to boil. Cool under cold running water, then peel and cut into quarters.

3 Heat the oil in a small non-stick frying pan over medium heat. Cook the bacon for 5 minutes, or until crisp. Drain on paper towels and allow to cool.

4 Combine the sour cream, mayonnaise, mustard and vinegar and mix until smooth. Add to the potatoes, along with the spring onion and most of the bacon. Season to taste with salt and freshly ground black pepper and gently toss to combine.

5 Top with the egg quarters and sprinkle with the remaining bacon. Serve at room temperature, or cover and refrigerate until required.

Each serving provides
1489 kJ, 355 kcal, 20 g protein, 21 g fat (6 g saturated fat), 21 g carbohydrate (2 g sugars), 3 g fibre, 729 mg sodium

Couscous and chickpea salad

Preparation 10 minutes

Cooking 10 minutes

For 1

¼ cup (45 g) instant couscous

1 tablespoon currants

1 tablespoon slivered almonds

1 tablespoon olive oil

¼ red onion, chopped

¼ capsicum (bell pepper), chopped

½ teaspoon ground cumin

¼ cup (30 g) canned chickpeas

3 pitted green olives, quartered

3 teaspoons chopped fresh parsley

2 teaspoons lemon juice

For 2

½ cup (95 g) instant couscous

2 tablespoons currants

2 tablespoons slivered almonds

2 tablespoons olive oil

½ red onion, chopped

½ capsicum (bell pepper), chopped

1 teaspoon ground cumin

½ cup (60 g) canned chickpeas

6 pitted green olives, quartered

1½ tablespoons chopped fresh parsley

1 tablespoon lemon juice

1 Place the couscous and currants in a heatproof bowl. Add ¼ cup (60 ml) boiling water if cooking for one, or ½ cup (125 ml) boiling water if cooking for two. Cover with foil and stand for 5 minutes, or until all the water is absorbed. Fluff the couscous with a fork to break up any lumps.

2 Meanwhile, toast the almonds in a dry, non-stick frying pan over medium heat for 3–4 minutes, or until lightly golden in colour, stirring occasionally. Remove from the pan.

3 Heat 2 teaspoons of the oil in the pan over medium heat. Add the onion and capsicum and cook, stirring, for 3–4 minutes, or until softened.

4 Add the cumin, chickpeas, olives, almonds, parsley, lemon juice and remaining oil. Stir the couscous through and season with salt and freshly ground black pepper. Serve immediately, or cover and refrigerate until required.

Leftover magic

Use any leftover chickpeas to make hummus. Blend them with crushed garlic, olive oil, tahini (sesame seed paste), ground cumin and lemon juice. Spread on sandwiches or use as a dip.

Each serving provides
1765 kJ, 422 kcal, 10 g protein, 23 g fat (3 g saturated fat), 44 g carbohydrate (3 g sugars), 4 g fibre, 79 mg sodium

This salad goes especially well with grilled chicken and fish, pan-fried lamb cutlets, or seared lamb backstraps or loin fillets.

Asian rice salad

Preparation 10 minutes

Cooking 15 minutes

Quick

For 1

⅓ cup (65 g) long-grain white rice

2 baby corn, sliced diagonally

4 snow peas (mangetout), sliced

¼ small red capsicum (bell pepper), chopped

1 stick celery, thinly sliced

1 spring onion (scallion), sliced

2 teaspoons vegetable oil

2 teaspoons salt-reduced soy sauce

2 teaspoons rice vinegar

¼ teaspoon grated fresh ginger

1 tablespoon cashew nuts

For 2

⅔ cup (135 g) long-grain white rice

4 baby corn, sliced diagonally

8 snow peas (mangetout), sliced

½ small red capsicum (bell pepper), chopped

2 sticks celery, thinly sliced

2 spring onions (scallions), sliced

1 tablespoon vegetable oil

1 tablespoon salt-reduced soy sauce

1 tablespoon rice vinegar

½ teaspoon grated fresh ginger

2 tablespoons cashew nuts

1 Cook the rice in a medium saucepan of boiling water for 10–12 minutes, or until just tender, adding the corn in the last 2 minutes of cooking. Drain and rinse under cold running water.

2 Place the rice in a salad bowl along with the snow peas, capsicum, celery and spring onion. Toss to combine.

3 Whisk together the oil, soy sauce, vinegar and ginger and pour over the salad. Toss together, sprinkle with the cashews and serve.

Cook's tip

Jasmine rice (Thai fragrant rice) works well for this recipe.

Other ideas

- Toss chopped fresh coriander (cilantro) through the salad.
- Add chopped fresh chilli or dried red chilli flakes to the dressing.
- Add sliced cooked chicken to the salad.

Each serving provides
1665 kJ, 398 kcal, 8 g protein, 13 g fat (2 g saturated fat), 59 g carbohydrate (3 g sugars), 3 g fibre, 400 mg sodium

Prosciutto, pear and parmesan salad

Preparation 10 minutes

Cooking None

For 1

½ cup (25 g) baby rocket
(arugula) leaves

½ pear, cored and thinly sliced

2 slices prosciutto, about 20 g
(¾ oz)

1½ tablespoons shaved
parmesan

2 teaspoons olive oil

1 teaspoon balsamic vinegar

For 2

1 cup (50 g) baby rocket
(arugula) leaves

1 pear, cored and thinly sliced

4 slices prosciutto, about 40 g
(1½ oz)

¼ cup (30 g) shaved parmesan

1 tablespoon olive oil

2 teaspoons balsamic vinegar

1 Place the rocket and pear in a serving bowl.
Tear the prosciutto into pieces and add to the
bowl along with the parmesan. Gently toss.

2 Whisk the oil and vinegar together and season
with salt and freshly ground black pepper. Drizzle
over the salad and serve immediately.

Serving suggestion

This elegant, simple salad is lovely with fresh,
crusty bread.

Another idea

Stir-fry the prosciutto until crisp, then break it
into pieces over the salad.

Each serving provides
1062 kJ, 254 kcal, 12 g protein, 17 g fat (6 g saturated fat),
13 g carbohydrate (10 g sugars), 2 g fibre, 484 mg sodium

Quick ideas for... salad leaves

Bags of multi-coloured mixed salad leaves and loose leaves sold by weight are so convenient, as you can buy as much or as little as you need. Take a bag or handful of leaves and try these sensational salads.

Salad leaf secrets

To prepare salad leaves, fill a large bowl or sink with cold water and submerge the leaves. (If using a whole lettuce, pull all the leaves apart first.) Soak for 5 minutes, then gently agitate the water with your hand and leave to settle again, so any dirt or grit in the leaves sinks to the bottom.

To dry the leaves, carefully lift handfuls of the leaves into a salad spinner, then spin to dry the leaves. Alternatively, put the leaves in a clean tea towel (dish towel), gather up the ends and shake in short, sharp motions over the sink, against your other hand.

Alternatively, try this method outside. Hold the gathered ends of the tea towel in your hand, then swing your arm around in windmill-fashion — the water from the leaves will be absorbed into the tea towel. Sounds strange, but it works!

Store in an airtight container in the fridge for up to 3 days (depending on the freshness of the lettuce).

Noodle salad

Cook a piece of **steak** to your liking (see page 148); allow to rest, then thinly slice. Meanwhile, soak **dried rice noodles** in boiling **water** for 5 minutes (or according to packet instructions). Drain, rinse under cold running water and drain well. Toss the noodles and steak with **mixed lettuce leaves**, blanched **snow peas** (mangetout), **shredded carrot** and quartered **cherry tomatoes**. Dress with **sweet chilli sauce** mixed with **lime juice** to taste.

Roasted vegetable salad

This is a great way to use up leftover roast vegetables, or roast up extra vegetables when the oven is already on. Roast chunks of **red onion**, **red capsicum** (bell pepper), **eggplant** (aubergine), **zucchini (courgette)** and **pumpkin** (winter squash) or **sweet potato** until tender and browned. Cool to room temperature, then mix in a bowl with baby **rocket** (arugula) leaves and crumbled **fetta**. Dress with **olive oil** and **balsamic** or **red wine vinegar.**

Chicken waldorf salad

In a bowl, toss together some thinly sliced **red apple**, shredded cooked **chicken**, sliced **celery**, chopped toasted **walnuts** and **lettuce leaves** — baby cos (romaine) lettuce is particularly good. Dress with **mayonnaise**, thinned down with **lemon juice** and a little water, to taste.

Prawn and potato salad

Dress cooked, cooled and halved small **new potatoes** with a little **olive oil** and **white wine vinegar** or **lemon juice**. Toss with **baby English spinach leaves**, peeled cooked **prawns** (shrimp), halved **cherry tomatoes** and sliced **spring onions** (scallions).

Egg and bacon salad

Hard-boil 1 or 2 **eggs**; allow to cool, then peel and quarter. Fry chopped **bacon** until crisp and drain on paper towel. Make a bed of **lettuce leaves** on a plate or plates. Top with the egg and bacon, some chopped **tomatoes** and finely sliced **red onion** or **spring onion (scallion)**. Dress with a little **red wine vinegar** and extra virgin **olive oil**.

Antipasto salad

Marinated vegetables are available by weight from most supermarket delicatessens. Toss **salad leaves** in a bowl with quartered **artichoke hearts**, roasted **red capsicum** (bell pepper), **chargrilled eggplant** (aubergine) and **marinated button mushrooms**. Add quartered **bocconcini** (fresh baby mozzarella balls) and sliced **salami** or **prosciutto**. Serve with **crusty bread**.

Grow your own

Instead of buying small amounts of salad leaves, the other solution is to grow your own. Even a small balcony can support several lettuces in pots. If you grow non-hearting varieties, you can simply pick the outer leaves as you need them, rather than having to harvest the whole plant. This also works well for herbs, rocket (arugula) and spinach.

Bean taco salad

Arrange a bed of **lettuce leaves** on a plate or plates. Top with rinsed canned **red kidney beans**, then drizzle with a little **taco sauce**. Layer grated **cheese**, diced **avocado**, diced **tomato** and finely chopped **red onion** on top. Add a dollop of **light sour cream** and serve with **corn chips**.

Fig, walnut and goat's cheese salad

Arrange **mixed salad leaves** on a plate or plates. Thickly slice 1 or 2 **fresh figs** crosswise and arrange over the leaves, then sprinkle with crumbled **goat's cheese** and **walnut pieces**. Drizzle with a dressing of **olive oil**, **lemon juice** and crushed **garlic** and serve with **crusty bread**.

Cook's tips

Use the meat from a barbecued or roasted chicken in this recipe.

Kecap manis is a thick, sweet Indonesian soy sauce. You'll find it in larger supermarkets.

Chicken and noodle salad

Preparation 10 minutes

Cooking 10 minutes

Quick

For 1

50 g (1¾ oz) rice stick noodles

½ Lebanese or other small cucumber

⅓ cup (60 g) shredded cooked chicken

¼ carrot, julienned

¼ small red capsicum (bell pepper), julienned

1 spring onion (scallion), diagonally sliced

3 fresh mint leaves, shredded

1 tablespoon roughly chopped coriander (cilantro) leaves

½ teaspoon vegetable oil

½ teaspoon kecap manis

1 teaspoon lime juice

1 teaspoon sweet chilli sauce

For 2

100 g (3½ oz) rice stick noodles

1 Lebanese or other small cucumber

⅔ cup (115 g) shredded cooked chicken

½ carrot, julienned

½ small red capsicum (bell pepper), julienned

2 spring onions (scallions), diagonally sliced

6 fresh mint leaves, shredded

2 tablespoons roughly chopped coriander (cilantro) leaves

1 teaspoon vegetable oil

1 teaspoon kecap manis

2 teaspoons lime juice

2 teaspoons sweet chilli sauce

1 Cook the noodles in a saucepan of boiling water for 6 minutes, or until softened. Drain well.

2 Meanwhile, cut the cucumber in half lengthwise and remove the seeds using a teaspoon. Cut the cucumber into long, thin strips. Place in a bowl with the chicken and the carrot, capsicum, spring onion, mint, coriander and noodles.

3 Whisk together the oil, kecap manis, lime juice and chilli sauce. Add to the salad and toss until well combined. Serve immediately.

Other ideas

- Use hokkien (egg) noodles instead of rice noodles. You won't need to boil them.
- Replace the chicken with cooked beef, cut into thin strips.

Each serving provides
1403 kJ, 335 kcal, 17 g protein, 7 g fat (1 g saturated fat), 50 g carbohydrate (6 g sugars), 3 g fibre, 343 mg sodium

Gado gado

Preparation 10 minutes

Cooking 20 minutes

For 1

1 small carrot

40 g (1½ oz) green beans

1 small desiree potato, about 100 g
  (3½ oz)

60 g (2 oz) wombok (Chinese
  cabbage), cut in wedges

25 g (1 oz) bean sprouts

1 boiled egg, peeled and quartered

¼ cup (60 g) satay sauce

For 2

2 small carrots

80 g (2¾ oz) green beans

2 small desiree potatoes, about
  100 g (3½ oz each)

120 g (4 oz) wombok (Chinese
  cabbage), cut in wedges

50 g (1¾ oz) bean sprouts

2 boiled eggs, peeled and quartered

½ cup (125 g) satay sauce

Each serving provides
2024 kJ, 485 kcal, 17 g protein, 36 g fat
(12 g saturated fat), 24 g carbohydrate
(13 g sugars), 8 g fibre, 515 mg sodium

Step 1   Trim the carrot and beans. Slice the carrot diagonally and cut the potato into quarters. Meanwhile, bring a pot of water to a boil over high heat. Add the carrot and cook for 4 minutes, or until just tender. Remove using a slotted spoon and refresh under cold water.

Step 2   Blanch the beans and wombok in the boiling water for 2 minutes; remove with a slotted spoon and refresh under cold water or in a bowl of cold water. Add the potato to the boiling water and cook for 8 minutes, or until tender. Drain.

If you wish to make your own satay sauce, it's quick and easy to prepare — see our recipe on page 245.

Step 3 — Meanwhile, trim the tails from the bean sprouts. Arrange the vegetables, sprouts and egg in piles on a serving plate. Serve drizzled with the satay sauce.

Duck salad

Preparation 10 minutes

Cooking 20 minutes

For 1

1 small duck breast

½ cup (15 g) watercress sprigs

½ cup (15 g) shredded radicchio

½ red apple, cored and thinly
sliced

1 spring onion (scallion), sliced
diagonally

2 teaspoons olive oil

1 teaspoon white wine vinegar

For 2

2 small duck breasts

1 cup (30 g) watercress sprigs

1 cup (30 g) shredded
radicchio

1 red apple, cored and thinly
sliced

2 spring onions (scallions),
sliced diagonally

1 tablespoon olive oil

2 teaspoons white wine vinegar

1 Preheat the oven to 190°C (375°F/Gas 5).

2 Heat an ovenproof non-stick frying pan over medium–low heat. Season the duck with salt and freshly ground black pepper and place in the pan, skin side down. Cook for 6–8 minutes, or until most of the fat has rendered and the skin is crisp. Turn and cook the other side for 1 minute.

3 Transfer the pan to the oven and cook for a further 6 minutes for medium, or until done to your liking. Set the duck aside to rest for a few minutes, then slice it.

4 Combine the watercress, radicchio, apple, spring onion and duck slices in a bowl.

5 Whisk together the oil and vinegar and season with salt and freshly ground black pepper. Pour the dressing over the salad, toss together gently and serve.

Other ideas

- Replace the duck with a cooked Peking duck breast from the supermarket.
- Use a boneless, skinless chicken breast instead of the duck breast.
- Instead of duck, you could also use slices of leftover cooked turkey.
- Instead of apple slices, use orange wedges.

Each serving provides
1175 kJ, 281 kcal, 26 g protein, 14 g fat (2 g saturated fat),
10 g carbohydrate (9 g sugars), 2 g fibre, 85 mg sodium

from one Ratatouille Pan-fried pork chops Roast chick

stard salmon THAI BEEF RED CURRY STEP-BY-STEP

eas with... lamb cutlets Tarragon chicken Fish

Step-by-step Crumbed chicken fillets MANY MEALS FROM ONE B

IDEAS FOR... STEAK Lamb and ginger stir-fry Grille

Spiced spatchcock Step-by-step Pan-roasted qua

Baked fish parcel TUNA STEAK WITH SALSA ROS

Many meals from one Beef stew

mini lamb roast with red wine gravy Pork

Greek-style lamb

mains

Many meals from one — ratatouille

A classic stew of summer vegetables, ratatouille is a splendid accompaniment to meat, chicken or fish. This simple version serves 8, so you can transform leftovers into enticing new meals.

Ratatouille

Makes 8 serves

Preparation 20 minutes

Cooking 30 minutes

2 tablespoons olive oil

1 large onion, chopped

3 cloves garlic, crushed

2 red capsicums (bell peppers), chopped

4 zucchini (courgettes), halved lengthwise and thickly sliced

3 eggplant (aubergine), chopped

2 x 410g (15 oz) cans chopped tomatoes

1 Heat the oil in a large heavy-based saucepan over medium heat. Add the onion and cook for 5 minutes, or until soft and lightly golden. Add the garlic and cook for 1 minute, then add the capsicums and cook for 2 minutes, stirring occasionally. Stir in the zucchini and eggplant until well combined.

2 Add the tomatoes and bring to a boil. Reduce the heat to low, partially cover with the lid, then simmer for 20 minutes, or until the vegetables are tender, stirring occasionally. Season with salt, freshly ground black pepper and a good pinch of sugar, to taste.

3 To freeze the ratatouille, cool it completely, then divide into portions for 1 or 2 and place in airtight containers or zip-lock bags. Label, date and freeze for up to 3 months. To use, thaw in the microwave, or overnight in the fridge.

You'll never be short of easy dinner options with some extra Ratatouille, Beef stew (page 154) or Bolognese sauce (page 160) in the fridge or freezer.

Ways to use ratatouille

The following recipes serve 2, and each uses two ratatouille portions. Halve the recipes to serve 1.

Spicy vegetarian chickpea stew

In a saucepan, gently heat the **ratatouille** and two rinsed, drained 125 g (4 oz) cans **chickpeas**. Stir in 1 cup (45 g) chopped **baby English spinach** and ½ teaspoon **dried red chilli flakes**, or to taste. Serve with a dollop of **yogurt** or **sour cream**, on a bed of **steamed rice**, if desired.

Tuna pasta bake

Preheat the oven to 200°C (400°F/Gas 6). Cook 100 g (3½ oz) **short pasta** (such as penne, spirals or farfalle) until al dente. Drain well, then return to the pan. Stir in the **ratatouille** and a 95 g (3¼ oz) can of drained and flaked **tuna**. Spread into a 5 cup (1.25 litre) baking dish and top with ½ cup (75 g) grated **mozzarella** or ½ cup (60 g) grated **cheddar**. Bake for 15 minutes, or until the cheese has melted and is bubbling.

Ratatouille tarts

Preheat the oven to 200°C (400°F/Gas 6) and line a baking tray with baking paper. Cut a sheet of frozen **puff pastry** in half. Tightly re-wrap one pastry half in plastic wrap and return to the freezer. Thaw the other half, cut into two squares and place on the baking tray. Use a small sharp knife to score a border 1 cm (½ inch) in from the edge, all the way around each piece. Prick the pastry inside the border with a fork, then bake for 15 minutes, until puffed and golden.

Meanwhile, reheat the **ratatouille**. Place each pastry square on a serving plate; if the pastry centre has puffed up, gently press it down with a clean tea towel (dish towel). Pile the ratatouille in the centre, crumble **fetta** over the top, sprinkle with **fresh thyme leaves** and serve immediately.

Curried lentil pasties (pies)

Preheat the oven to 200°C (400°F/Gas 6). Reheat the **ratatouille** in a small saucepan. Add ¼ cup (60 g) **red lentils**, ¼ cup (60 ml) **water** and 1 teaspoon **curry powder**. Cover and bring to a simmer, then reduce the heat to very low. Cook for 15 minutes, or until the lentils are tender, stirring regularly so they don't stick to the pan. Allow to cool completely.

Meanwhile, thaw 2 sheets frozen **shortcrust pastry**. Using a bowl as a guide, cut a 15 cm (6 inch) diameter round from one corner of the pastry, then cut a round from the opposite corner: it will overlap where you have already cut, so use a leftover pastry scrap to patch the gap.

Spoon the lentil mixture onto the pastry rounds. Gather the pastry up, pinch firmly to seal, then press down gently so the pasties have a flat base. Bake for 20 minutes, until golden brown.

Ratatouille with polenta

Reheat the **ratatouille** in a small saucepan. In another pan, heat 1⅓ cups (330 ml) **chicken or vegetable stock** until boiling; add ½ cup (75 g) **instant polenta** and stir over low heat for 3 minutes, or until thick and soft. Stir in 2 tablespoons grated **parmesan**. Serve the ratatouille over the polenta, sprinkled with **fresh basil**. Also good topped with a **poached egg**.

Ratatouille with baked fish

Preheat the oven to 200°C (400°F/Gas 6). Spread the **ratatouille** in a 20 x 15 cm (8 x 6 inch) baking dish. Arrange two 150 g (5 oz) **salmon or white fish fillets** on top. Drizzle with 2 teaspoons **olive oil** and 2 teaspoons **lemon juice**, then season with **salt** and freshly ground **black pepper**. Bake for 15 minutes, or until the fish is cooked.

Grilled fish with lime and ginger butter

Preparation 10 minutes

Cooking 15 minutes

For 1

1½ tablespoons softened butter

½ teaspoon very finely chopped kaffir lime (makrut) leaves

½ teaspoon grated fresh ginger

½ teaspoon very finely chopped red chilli

1 teaspoon finely chopped coriander (cilantro)

200 g (7 oz) ling fillet

olive oil, for drizzling

For 2

3 tablespoons softened butter

1 teaspoon very finely chopped kaffir lime (makrut) leaves

1 teaspoon grated fresh ginger

1 teaspoon very finely chopped red chilli

2 teaspoons finely chopped coriander (cilantro)

2 x 200 g (7 oz) ling fillets

olive oil, for drizzling

Each serving provides
1942 kJ, 464 kcal, 40 g protein, 34 g fat (17 g saturated fat), 1 g carbohydrate (<1 g sugars), <1 g fibre, 491 mg sodium

1 Combine the butter, lime leaves, ginger, chilli and coriander in a small bowl. Place the mixture on a piece of plastic wrap and roll into a thick log. Secure with plastic wrap and refrigerate until firm.

2 Meanwhile, preheat the grill (broiler) to medium–high. Line a baking tray with baking (parchment) paper. Place the fish on the baking tray, drizzle with olive oil and season with salt and freshly ground black pepper.

3 Grill (broil) the fish for 6 minutes on each side, or until opaque and just cooked through. (Alternatively, fry the fish on a chargrill pan for about 3 minutes on each side.)

4 Top the fish with slices of the lime and ginger butter. Serve with a salad or lightly grilled or steamed vegetables.

Cook's tips

■ Ling is an ideal fish for grilling as it holds its shape well. You can use any firm white fish fillets, or even trout or salmon.

■ Lime leaves are sometimes sold loose, so you can buy small portions. They can also be frozen and used in curries — there is no need to thaw them first.

Other ideas

Try these other herb variations for the butter:

■ tarragon and grated lemon zest

■ garlic and parsley

■ basil and chives

■ lemon and dill.

Cook's tip

You can make enough garlic butter for a whole baguette, then simply cut the baguette into portions and freeze what are you are not going to cook. Later just reheat the frozen baguette in the oven to accompany another baked meal.

Other ideas

Use any white firm fish or fresh tuna. Top with:

- finely grated lime zest, lime slices and some snipped fresh chives or coriander (cilantro); also enclose some zucchini (courgette) batons or slices in the parcel
- sliced French or Asian shallots, sliced fresh ginger, crushed garlic and sweet soy sauce; enclose some halved baby bok choy as well.

Baked fish parcel

Preparation 10 minutes

Cooking 25 minutes

For 1

175 g (6 oz) salmon fillet

2–3 sprigs fresh thyme

½ lemon, cut into thin slices

1 teaspoon capers

1 tablespoon chopped fresh parsley

1 teaspoon olive oil

7 cm (2¾ inch) length of baguette

½ tablespoon butter

½ clove garlic, finely grated

125 g (4 oz) cherry tomatoes on the vine

For 2

2 x 175 g (6 oz) salmon fillets

3–4 sprigs fresh thyme

1 lemon, cut into thin slices

2 teaspoons capers

2 tablespoon chopped fresh parsley

2 teaspoons olive oil

15 cm (6 inch) length of baguette

1 tablespoon butter

1 clove garlic, finely grated

250 g (8 oz) cherry tomatoes on the vine

1 Preheat the oven to 200°C (400°F/Gas 6).

2 For each piece of fish, place a 30 x 30 cm (12 x 12 inch) piece of foil on a clean surface; place a square of baking paper of top. Place the fish in the middle. Top with the thyme sprigs, lemon slices, capers and parsley and drizzle with some of the olive oil. Season with salt and freshly ground black pepper.

3 Carefully wrap each parcel, bringing the edges of the foil to the centre and folding down firmly to secure the top and the sides.

4 Cut the baguette in half lengthwise. Combine the butter and garlic and spread the mixture down the centre of the baguette. Wrap the bread in foil.

5 Place each fish parcel on a lined baking tray, with the garlic bread and cherry tomatoes alongside. Drizzle the tomatoes with the remaining olive oil and season with salt and pepper. Bake for 20 minutes for medium-cooked fish, or 25 minutes if you prefer it well done. Serve with a simple green salad or salad leaves.

Each serving provides
2515 kJ, 601 kcal, 42 g protein, 28 g fat (8 g saturated fat), 44 g carbohydrate (7 g sugars), 6 g fibre, 615 mg sodium

Fish baked with lentils

Preparation 5 minutes

Cooking 40 minutes

For 1

200 g (7 oz) can lentils, drained

1 small tomato, roughly diced

¼ cup (40 g) sliced roasted red capsicum (bell pepper)

1 bay leaf

1 sprig fresh thyme

2 tablespoons chicken stock or white wine

200 g (7 oz) perch or other firm white fish fillet

2 teaspoons chopped fresh parsley

For 2

400 g (14 oz) can lentils, drained

1 tomato, roughly diced

½ cup (80 g) sliced roasted red capsicum (bell pepper)

2 bay leaves

2 sprigs fresh thyme

¼ cup (60 ml) chicken stock or white wine

2 x 200 g (7 oz) perch or other firm white fish fillets

1 tablespoon chopped fresh parsley

1 Preheat the oven to 180°C (350°F/Gas 4).

2 Put the lentils, tomato, capsicum, bay leaf, thyme and stock in a 1 litre (4 cup) casserole dish and lightly combine. Cover tightly with foil and bake for 20 minutes.

3 Remove the dish from the oven and remove the foil. Place the fish flat on top of the lentils and bake for a further 20 minutes, or until the fish is cooked through.

4 Serve the fish on a bed of lentils, drizzled with the baking juices and sprinkled with the parsley and freshly ground black pepper.

Cook's tip

Leftover chicken stock can be frozen in ice cube trays to use in sauces or other dishes. Stock (bouillon) cubes or powder are a convenient alternative to liquid stock.

Other ideas

- Use any firm white fish fillets — just make sure any bones are removed.
- Add some sliced black olives and capers to the lentil mixture.
- Serve with rice or crusty bread, and lightly dressed baby spinach or salad leaves.

Each serving provides
1135 kJ, 271 kcal, 41 g protein, 3 g fat (<1 g saturated fat), 14 g carbohydrate (4 g sugars), 5 g fibre, 485 mg sodium

This healthy dish is quick to prepare but takes a while to bake. You could bake some potato slices or wedges in the oven at the same time as the fish.

Leftover magic

Refrigerate any leftover beans in an airtight container and use in the next few days to make another 'mash' to serve with other grilled fish or meats. Vary the flavour by adding different chopped fresh herbs; instead of spinach leaves, try baby rocket (arugula), thinly sliced zucchini (courgette) or finely chopped fresh fennel.

Other ideas

■ Cook the salmon in the same way, but serve it on a large, lightly toasted sourdough roll with some mayonnaise and your favourite salad fillings.

■ Alternatively, flake the warm salmon into big chunks and serve it in your favourite salad.

■ Marinating the salmon for a few hours or overnight will also maximise the flavour.

Honey mustard salmon

Preparation 10 minutes

Cooking 10 minutes

For 1

1 teaspoon vegetable oil

1 teaspoon soy sauce

½ teaspoon honey

½ teaspoon wholegrain mustard

2 teaspoons lemon juice, plus some grated lemon zest

1 x 125 g (4 oz) skinless salmon fillet

½ x 400 g (14 oz) can butter beans (lima beans)

1 small clove garlic, crushed

2 teaspoons extra virgin olive oil

a pinch of dried red chilli flakes

1 cup (50 g) baby English spinach leaves

4 vine-ripened cherry tomatoes

For 2

2 teaspoons vegetable oil

2 teaspoons soy sauce

1 teaspoon honey

1 teaspoon wholegrain mustard

1 tablespoon lemon juice, plus some grated lemon zest

2 x 125 g (4 oz) skinless salmon fillets

1 x 400 g (14 oz) can butter beans (lima beans)

1 clove garlic, crushed

1 tablespoon extra virgin olive oil

a pinch of dried red chilli flakes

2 cups (100 g) baby English spinach leaves

8 vine-ripened cherry tomatoes

1 In a shallow dish, combine the vegetable oil, soy sauce, honey, mustard and half the lemon juice. Add the salmon and coat all over.

2 Drain and rinse the beans. Place in a saucepan with the garlic, oil, chilli flakes, remaining lemon juice and lemon zest and gently heat through. Roughly crush the beans using a vegetable masher or fork, then stir in the spinach and season with salt and freshly ground black pepper. Gently heat until the spinach wilts.

3 Meanwhile, heat a non-stick frying pan or grill pan until hot. Cook the salmon for 2–3 minutes on each side, or until just firm and pink, adding the tomatoes during the last 1–2 minutes to warm them through.

4 Serve the salmon on the beans, with the tomatoes and extra lemon wedges if desired.

Each serving provides
2005 kJ, 479 kcal, 36 g protein, 24 g fat (4 g saturated fat), 25 g carbohydrate (9 g sugars), 10 g fibre, 575 mg sodium

Tuna steak with salsa rossa

Preparation 10 minutes

Cooking 15 minutes

For 1

2 teaspoons olive oil

½ teaspoon red wine vinegar

1 x 150 g (5 oz) tuna steak

8 thin green beans, halved

3 pitted black olives, halved

4 fresh basil leaves

Salsa rossa

2 teaspoons olive oil

1 spring onion (scallion), sliced

½ red chilli, seeds removed, flesh finely chopped

1 small clove garlic, finely chopped

a tiny pinch of cinnamon

a small pinch of sugar

1 vine-ripened tomato, peeled (see tip) and diced

1 thick roasted red capsicum (bell pepper) strip (from the deli or a jar), diced

½ teaspoon red wine vinegar

For 2

1 tablespoon olive oil

1 teaspoon red wine vinegar

2 x 150 g (5 oz) tuna steaks

16 thin green beans, halved

6 pitted black olives, halved

8 fresh basil leaves

Salsa rossa

3 teaspoons olive oil

2 spring onions (scallions), sliced

1 red chilli, seeds removed, flesh finely chopped

1 clove garlic, finely chopped

a small pinch of cinnamon

a pinch of sugar

2 vine-ripened tomatoes, peeled (see tip) and diced

2 thick roasted red capsicum (bell pepper) strips (from the deli or a jar), diced

1 teaspoon red wine vinegar

Each serving provides
1854 kJ, 443 kcal, 41 g protein, 27 g fat (6 g saturated fat), 8 g carbohydrate (6 g sugars), 4 g fibre, 211 mg sodium

Other ideas

■ Replace the basil with fresh mint leaves.

▨ Instead of the tomato, use some cherry tomatoes — you won't need to peel them.

How to peel a tomato

To peel a tomato, turn it upside down, then score a cross into the skin using a small sharp knife. Place in a small bowl and cover with boiling water. After about 30 seconds, carefully lift it out of the water and allow it to cool a little. Then simply pull the skin away from the cross — it should peel off easily.

1 Combine the oil and vinegar. Brush over both sides of the tuna and season with black pepper. (If you have time, let the tuna marinate briefly.)

2 Heat a non-stick frying pan over medium–high heat. Add the tuna and cook for 1 minute on each side, or until lightly browned but still very rare in the middle. Remove and set aside.

3 To make the salsa rossa, heat the oil in the same pan. Fry the spring onion for 1 minute over medium heat, until softened. Stir in the chilli, garlic, cinnamon and sugar. Add the tomato, capsicum and vinegar and bring to a boil.

4 Add the beans, then cover and simmer for 3 minutes. Stir in the olives and place the tuna over the top. Cover and cook for 3 minutes, or until the tuna is done to your liking and the beans are just tender.

5 Transfer the beans and tuna to a plate. Roughly tear the basil leaves and stir half into the warm salsa mixture, letting it bubble for a moment. Spoon the salsa over the tuna, scatter the remaining basil on top and serve.

Portuguese prawns

Preparation 10 minutes

Cooking 5 minutes

For 1

250 g (9 oz) raw prawns (uncooked shrimp)

1 tablespoon butter

2 teaspoons olive oil

½ small chilli, sliced

1 small clove garlic, crushed

1 tablespoon white wine

1 spring onion (scallion), finely chopped

For 2

500 g (1 lb) raw prawns (uncooked shrimp)

2 tablespoons butter

1 tablespoon olive oil

1 small red chilli, sliced

1 large clove garlic, crushed

2 tablespoons white wine

2 spring onions (scallions), finely chopped

Each serving provides
1934 kJ, 462 kcal, 52 g protein, 26 g fat
(12 g saturated fat), 1 g carbohydrate
(1 g sugars), 1 g fibre, 1019 mg sodium

Step 1 — Peel the prawns, leaving the tail on, then devein them.

Step 2 — Butterfly the prawns by slicing them lengthwise down the centre, being careful not to cut all the way through.

Frozen peeled prawns can also be used in this dish. Defrost them in small amounts for a quick, easy meal.

Step 3 Heat the butter and oil in a frying pan over medium–high heat. Add the prawns and cook for 2 minutes, turning once with tongs. Add the remaining ingredients and cook for 1 minute, or until the prawns are pink and curled. Serve with crusty bread and a green salad.

Scrub mussels on the outside and remove the beards before cooking. Discard any mussels that do not open after cooking as they may cause food poisoning.

Mussels with tomato and chorizo

Preparation 10 minutes

Cooking 15 minutes

For 1

1 teaspoon olive oil

40 g (1½ oz) chorizo sausage

½ small onion, finely chopped

1 clove garlic, crushed

½ teaspoon smoked paprika

2 small bay leaves

1 tomato, roughly chopped

¼ cup (60 ml) white wine

½ tablespoon fresh oregano

500 g (1 lb) mussels, in the shell

2 tablespoons cream

2 tablespoons chopped fresh parsley

crusty bread, to serve

For 2

2 teaspoons olive oil

80 g (2¾ oz) chorizo sausage

1 small onion, finely chopped

2 cloves garlic, crushed

1 teaspoon smoked paprika

3–4 bay leaves

2 tomatoes, roughly chopped

½ cup (125 ml) white wine

1 tablespoon fresh oregano

1 kg (2 lb) mussels, in the shell

¼ cup (60 ml) cream

2 tablespoons chopped fresh parsley

crusty bread, to serve

1 Heat the oil in a large saucepan over medium–high heat. Finely slice the chorizo and cook for 2–3 minutes, or until crisp. Remove from the pan using a slotted spoon and drain.

2 Sauté the onion in the pan for 2 minutes. Add the garlic and sauté for 1 minute. Add the paprika, bay leaves, tomato, wine and oregano and simmer for 5 minutes.

3 Add the mussels, then cover and cook for a further 5 minutes, or until the mussels have opened. Discard any mussels that don't open.

4 Fold the cream, parsley and chorizo through the mixture. Serve in a bowl, with crusty bread.

Other ideas

- For a South-East Asian twist, make a broth base from ingredients such as ginger, garlic, lemongrass, chillies, coconut milk and lots of lime juice.
- Replace the mussels with pippies or clams (vongole). They take about 3–4 minutes to cook and open.

Each serving provides
2149 kJ, 513 kcal, 40 g protein, 28 g fat (13 g saturated fat), 19 g carbohydrate (5 g sugars), 3 g fibre, 1429 mg sodium

Roast baby chicken with vegetables

Preparation 10 minutes

Cooking 50 minutes

For 1

olive oil, for brushing

1 potato, peeled and quartered

1 turnip, peeled and cut lengthwise

1 carrot, peeled and cut lengthwise

2 teaspoons butter, softened

½ teaspoon grated lemon zest

1 teaspoon finely chopped fresh tarragon

400 g (14 oz) spatchcock chicken (poussin)

For 2

olive oil, for brushing

2 potatoes, peeled and quartered

2 turnips, peeled and cut lengthwise

2 carrots, peeled and cut lengthwise

1 tablespoon butter, softened

1 teaspoon grated lemon zest

2 teaspoons finely chopped fresh tarragon

2 x 400 g (14 oz) spatchcock chickens (poussin)

1 Preheat the oven to 200°C (400°F/Gas 6). Grease a baking tray with oil, place the vegetables on the tray and drizzle with some more oil. Season with salt and freshly ground black pepper and bake for 15 minutes.

2 Meanwhile, combine the butter, lemon zest and tarragon in a small bowl. Pat the chicken dry with paper towels. Gently separate the skin on top of the breast from the chicken. Place the tarragon butter under the skin, being careful not to break the skin. Secure with a toothpick.

3 Place the chicken on the baking tray, with the vegetables. Bake for 30–35 minutes, or until the juices run clear when the chicken's leg is pierced.

Another idea

If you have leftover fresh breadcrumbs, make a stuffing for the bird. For each person, mix ½ cup (40 g) breadcrumbs with 2 teaspoons chopped semi-dried (sun-blushed) tomatoes, some chopped olives, a sprinkling of fetta and chopped fresh basil. Stuff the mixture into the bird before roasting.

Leftover magic

A 400 g (14 oz) bird will give you a generous serving. Any extra meat can be used in salads, sandwiches or an omelette the next day.

Each serving provides
2933 kJ, 701 kcal, 42 g protein, 48 g fat (16 g saturated fat), 24 g carbohydrate (8 g sugars), 7 g fibre, 292 mg sodium

A chicken Maryland is the thigh and drumstick cut in one piece, and still on the bone. If you can't get this cut, use a thigh and a drumstick.

Roast chicken Maryland

Preparation 15 minutes

Cooking 45 minutes

For 1

½ small lemon

2 teaspoons softened butter

1 teaspoon fresh thyme

1 chicken Maryland

1 small carrot, peeled

1 small parsnip, peeled

olive oil spray

50 g (1¾ oz) green beans, trimmed

For 2

1 small lemon

1 tablespoon softened butter

2 teaspoons fresh thyme

2 chicken Marylands

2 small carrots, peeled

2 small parsnips, peeled

olive oil spray

100 g (3½ oz) green beans, trimmed

1 Preheat the oven to 180°C (350°F/Gas 4). Finely grate the lemon zest into a small bowl. Add the butter and thyme and mix to combine. Use your fingers to ease the skin from the chicken, being careful not to tear it, then spread the butter mixture under the skin.

2 Place the chicken in a baking dish. Cut each carrot and parsnip into 4–5 pieces and arrange around the chicken. Squeeze the lemon juice over the chicken, then spray the chicken and vegetables with a little olive oil. Season with salt and freshly ground black pepper.

3 Roast for 40 minutes, turning the vegetables halfway through cooking. Near the end of roasting time, place the beans in a heatproof bowl, cover with boiling water, leave to stand for 2 minutes, then drain.

4 Add the beans to the baking dish and spray with a little olive oil. Roast for a final 3 minutes, or until the juices from the chicken run clear when the thickest part of the thigh is pierced with a skewer, and the vegetables are tender and browned. Serve the chicken and vegetables with the pan juices spooned over.

Each serving provides
2721 kJ, 650 kcal, 47 g protein, 46 g fat (17 g saturated fat), 11 g carbohydrate (7 g sugars), 5 g fibre, 336 mg sodium

Tarragon chicken

Preparation 10 minutes

Cooking 10 minutes

For 1

1 teaspoon vegetable oil

1 teaspoon butter

3 chicken tenderloins (tenders), about 175 g (6 oz) in total

1 spring onion (scallion), white part only, finely chopped

1 small clove garlic, crushed

2 teaspoons dry sherry

¼ cup (60 ml) pouring cream

¼ teaspoon dried tarragon

For 2

2 teaspoons vegetable oil

2 teaspoons butter

6 chicken tenderloins (tenders), about 350 g (12 oz) in total

2 spring onions (scallion), white part only, finely chopped

1 clove garlic, crushed

1 tablespoon dry sherry

½ cup (125 ml) pouring cream

½ teaspoon dried tarragon

1 Heat the oil and butter in a frying pan over medium heat. Fry the chicken for 3 minutes on each side, or until golden brown and cooked through. Remove the chicken to a plate.

2 Reduce the heat to medium–low. Add the onion and garlic to the pan and cook, stirring, for 30 seconds, or until soft. Gradually add the combined sherry and cream, stirring and scraping the pan with a wooden spoon.

3 Stir in the tarragon, reduce the heat to low and simmer for 2 minutes, or until the sauce has reduced slightly.

4 Return the chicken to the pan and turn to coat in the sauce. Allow to reheat briefly if needed, then serve.

Serving suggestion

This simple dish is fabulous with lightly steamed vegetables, such as asparagus, yellow button squash and green beans.

Cook's tips

- Dried herbs are convenient for use in small quantities, as fresh herbs don't keep very long.
- Look for 'light cooking cream' if you'd like to reduce the fat content of this dish.

Each serving provides
2382 kJ, 569 kcal, 39 g protein, 44 g fat (23 g saturated fat), 3 g carbohydrate (3 g sugars), <1 g fibre, 161 mg sodium

Sauté hints and tips

■ Make sure your pan is preheated, and the oil or butter is also hot before you add the food, so it begins to cook immediately. The pan needs to be hot enough so the food will sear nicely, but not so hot that the food burns before cooking through.

■ Make sure the food you are cooking isn't too wet, as this can hinder browning. To prevent this, moist ingredients such as fish can be lightly dusted with flour before cooking.

■ Don't overcrowd food in the pan, or the temperature will drop and the food will stew. Use a reasonable sized pan, even for a small amount of food.

Cook's tips

Toast the almonds in a dry frying pan over medium heat for about 1 minute, stirring often, until lightly golden.

Moroccan seasoning is a popular spice blend that is available at most supermarkets.

Pan-roasted quail with couscous

Preparation 15 minutes

Cooking 15 minutes

For 1

- 1 large quail, about 200 g (7 oz)
- ½ teaspoon Moroccan seasoning
- 2 teaspoons olive oil
- ⅓ cup (80 ml) chicken stock
- 50 g (1¾ oz) green beans, finely sliced diagonally
- ¼ cup (45 g) instant couscous
- 1½ tablespoons chopped dried apricots
- 1 tablespoon toasted slivered almonds
- 2 teaspoons chopped fresh coriander (cilantro) or chives (optional)

For 2

- 2 large quails, about 200 g (7 oz) each
- 1 teaspoon Moroccan seasoning
- 1 tablespoon olive oil
- ⅔ cup (150 ml) chicken stock
- 100 g (3½ oz) green beans, finely sliced diagonally
- ½ cup (95 g) instant couscous
- ¼ cup (45 g) chopped dried apricots
- 2 tablespoons toasted slivered almonds
- 1 tablespoon chopped fresh coriander (cilantro) or chives (optional)

1 Set each quail on a board, breast side down. Using kitchen scissors, cut down along each side of the backbone, then pull out and discard the backbone. Open out each quail and cut it in half between the breasts. Sprinkle the skin with the Moroccan seasoning.

2 Heat half the oil in a heavy-based frying pan over medium heat. Add the quail or quails, skin side down, and cook for 5 minutes, or until the skin is brown. Turn each quail over, so the browned side is up, then cover and cook for a further 7 minutes, or until cooked through.

3 Meanwhile, put the stock in a small saucepan. Cover and bring to a boil, then turn off the heat.

Lift the lid and quickly add the beans, couscous and apricots. Replace the lid and swirl the pan briefly to combine. Stand for 5 minutes to allow the couscous to absorb the stock.

4 Uncover the couscous, drizzle with the remaining oil and fluff up the grains with a fork. Cool slightly, then mix in the almonds. Serve the quail over the couscous, sprinkled with the coriander or chives if desired.

Each serving provides
3009 kJ, 719 kcal, 49 g protein, 37 g fat (7 g saturated fat), 48 g carbohydrate (10 g sugars), 5 g fibre, 568 mg sodium

Prosciutto-stuffed chicken

Preparation 15 minutes

Cooking 30 minutes

For 1

- 1 boneless, skinless chicken breast
- 1 slice prosciutto, chopped
- 2 tablespoons creamy goat's cheese
- 1 small slice roasted red capsicum (bell pepper), chopped
- 2 basil leaves (optional)

For 2

- 2 boneless, skinless chicken breasts
- 2 slices prosciutto, chopped
- $\frac{1}{3}$ cup (45 g) creamy goat's cheese
- 2 small slices roasted red capsicum (bell pepper), chopped
- 4 basil leaves (optional)

1 Preheat the oven to 200°C (400°F/Gas 6). Pound the chicken between two sheets of plastic wrap until about 5 mm (¼ inch) thick. Season on both sides with salt and freshly ground black pepper, then lay out the chicken with the short side facing you.

2 Mix the prosciutto through the goat's cheese, then spread over the chicken. Arrange the capsicum on top, then the basil leaves, if using.

3 Starting at a short end, roll up the meat gently, keeping the stuffing tucked in. Take care not to overfill or roll too tightly, or the parcel may split as it cooks. Secure with toothpicks, then place in a small greased baking dish, seam side down. Bake, uncovered, for 25–30 minutes, or until the chicken is cooked through.

4 Remove the toothpicks and cut the chicken on the diagonal, into slices. Serve drizzled with the pan juices.

Serving suggestion

Serve with a warm salad made from leftover roasted vegetables, fresh mixed salad leaves, and dressed with a splash of olive oil.

Each serving provides
1781 kJ, 425 kcal, 65 g protein, 18 g fat (6 g saturated fat), <1 g carbohydrate (<1 g sugars), <1 g fibre, 332 mg sodium

Other ideas

- Replace the prosciutto with chopped ham or cooked lean bacon.
- Instead of using the basil leaves, add some finely chopped fresh herbs to the cheese mixture, such as chives, sage and parsley.
- Try fetta, cream cheese or jarlsberg instead of the goat's cheese.
- Roast some vegetables with the chicken, such as asparagus spears, julienned carrots, fennel wedges, zucchini (courgette) chunks or sweet potato batons.

Other ideas

- For extra crunch, make fresh breadcrumbs from day-old bread. Simply tear the bread into pieces and whizz in a food processor until coarse crumbs form. Or try the coarse, dry Japanese breadcrumbs known as panko.

- Spread the cooked crumbed chicken with tomato pasta sauce, sprinkle with grated cheese and melt under a hot grill (broiler).

Leftover magic

These are great to have on hand in the freezer — make a double quantity, then place the crumbed chicken in zip-lock bags in serving portions. Lie the portions flat, expel the excess air, seal tightly and freeze for up to 6 months. Thaw them overnight in the fridge, then cook as directed. Only crumb and freeze chicken that has not been previously frozen.

Crumbed chicken fillets

For 2

Preparation 20 minutes

Cooking 10 minutes

1 Use a large sharp knife to cut the chicken in half horizontally, then cut each half into two pieces. Use a rolling pin to beat each piece to an even thickness of about 1 cm (½ inch). Spread the flour and breadcrumbs on separate plates, and lightly beat the eggs in a shallow bowl.

2 Coat each piece of chicken in the flour and shake off the excess. Dip the chicken into the egg, then into the breadcrumbs, pressing them on gently. Place in a single layer on a plate.

3 Heat about 1 cm (½ inch) oil in a frying pan over medium heat. Cook the chicken for 3–4 minutes on each side, or until golden brown and cooked through — don't have the heat too high, or the crumbs will over-brown before the chicken is fully cooked. Drain on paper towels.

4 Wipe out most of the oil from the pan. Increase the heat to medium–high and add the tomato. Cook for 1 minute on each side, until just seared. Season with salt and freshly ground black pepper. Serve with the chicken and a green salad, with lemon wedges to squeeze over.

1 large boneless, skinless chicken breast, about 300 g (10 oz)

2 tablespoons plain (all-purpose) flour

⅓ cup (35 g) dry packaged breadcrumbs

2 eggs

vegetable oil, for shallow frying

2 roma (plum) tomatoes, thickly sliced

green salad, to serve

lemon wedges, to serve

Each serving provides
1640 kJ, 392 kcal, 43 g protein, 14 g fat (4 g saturated fat), 22 g carbohydrate (2 g sugars), 2 g fibre, 294 mg sodium

For extra flavour, you can add grated parmesan or chopped fresh herbs such as parsley, thyme or rosemary to the breadcrumbs.

Seared duck breast with orange sauce

Preparation 10 minutes

Cooking 20 minutes

For 1

1 potato, about 150 g (5 oz)

1 teaspoon olive oil

1 duck breast

2 tablespoons orange juice

1 teaspoon shredded orange zest

1 tablespoon medium-dry sherry

1 small sprig rosemary

mixed salad leaves, to serve

For 2

2 potatoes, about 150 g (5 oz) each

2 teaspoons olive oil

2 duck breasts

$\frac{1}{3}$ cup (80 ml) orange juice

1 teaspoon shredded orange zest

2 tablespoons medium-dry sherry

1 small sprig rosemary

mixed salad leaves, to serve

1 Preheat the oven to 180°C (350°F/Gas 4). Peel each potato, cut into 3 cm (1¼ inch) pieces and cook in a small saucepan of boiling water for 5 minutes, or until just tender. Drain well.

2 Meanwhile, heat the oil in a frying pan over medium–high heat. Cook the duck, skin side down, for 2 minutes, or until golden. Reserving the frying pan, transfer the duck to a baking tray, skin side up. Bake for 10 minutes, then remove from the oven and leave to rest for 5 minutes.

3 While the duck is baking, reheat the oil and pan juices over medium heat. Add the potato and cook, turning, for 10 minutes, or until golden all over.

4 While the duck is resting, combine the orange juice, orange zest, sherry and rosemary in a small saucepan. Bring to a boil and cook for 3 minutes, or until the sauce has reduced by half. Slice the duck, drizzle with sauce, and serve with potato and salad leaves.

Another idea

To make honey–ginger glazed duck, omit the potatoes and cook the duck as above. While the duck is baking, discard all but about 1 teaspoon of fat from the frying pan. Reheat over medium heat, and for each person stir in ½ teaspoon grated ginger (from a jar is easy), 1 teaspoon honey, ¼ cup (60 ml) chicken stock and 1 teaspoon soy sauce. Bring to a boil and cook until reduced slightly. Serve with rice and steamed green vegetables.

Each serving provides
3318 kJ, 792 kcal, 25 g protein, 64 g fat (18 g saturated fat), 24 g carbohydrate (4 g sugars), 3 g fibre, 12 mg sodium

Even if you're cooking for one, this hearty dish is so good and freezes so well that it is worth making double, as it takes no extra time or effort.

Chicken cacciatore

For 2

Preparation 15 minutes

- -

Cooking 45 minutes

1 Heat the oil in a heavy-based saucepan or casserole dish over medium–high heat. Sprinkle the chicken with freshly ground black pepper. Brown the chicken until golden all over, about 3 minutes on each side. Transfer to a plate.

2 Reduce the heat to medium and add the onion, celery, carrot, mushrooms and bacon to the pan. Fry for about 5 minutes, or until the mushrooms are soft.

3 Pour in the wine or stock, reduce the heat to medium–low and simmer for 1 minute. Stir in the tomatoes, bay leaf, rosemary and parsley sprigs and paprika.

4 Return the chicken to the pan. Cover and simmer for 30 minutes, or until the juices run clear when tested with a skewer. Remove the bay leaf and rosemary and parsley sprigs. Sprinkle the chicken with chopped parsley and serve with crusty bread.

Other ideas

- Use chicken drumsticks instead of thighs, and pancetta instead of bacon.
- Sauté some crushed garlic with the vegetables in step 2.
- Stir in some pitted black olives or roasted red capsicum (bell pepper) strips in step 3.
- Toss some baby spinach leaves through the stew just before serving.

Leftover magic

Enjoy any leftover chicken for lunch or dinner within the next two days, perhaps on a bed of rice or pasta. Alternatively, freeze the chicken mixture in a small airtight container for up to 2 months.

1 tablespoon olive oil

4 bone-in skinless chicken thighs

1 small onion, chopped

1 celery stalk, thinly sliced

1 carrot, chopped

125 g (4 oz) button mushrooms, quartered

1 slice rindless bacon (bacon strip), finely diced

¼ cup (60 ml) dry red wine or chicken stock

400 g (14 oz) can crushed tomatoes

1 bay leaf

1 sprig fresh rosemary

3 sprigs fresh parsley, plus extra chopped parsley, to garnish

a pinch of paprika

crusty bread, to serve

- -

Each serving provides
1394 kJ, 333 kcal, 29 g protein, 17 g fat
(4 g saturated fat), 11 g carbohydrate
(9 g sugars), 6 g fibre, 551 mg sodium

Chicken and mushroom pot pie

Preparation 20 minutes

Cooking 30 minutes

For 1

1 teaspoon vegetable oil

200 g (7 oz) boneless, skinless chicken thighs, trimmed and chopped

1 slice rindless bacon (bacon strip), chopped

1 spring onion (scallion), chopped

50 g (1¾ oz) button mushrooms, chopped

1 teaspoon butter

1 teaspoon plain (all-purpose) flour

¼ cup (60 ml) milk, plus extra for brushing

2 tablespoons mixed frozen peas and corn, thawed slightly

¼ sheet frozen puff pastry

For 2

1 teaspoon vegetable oil

400 g (14 oz) boneless, skinless chicken thighs, trimmed and chopped

2 slices rindless bacon (bacon strips), chopped

2 spring onions (scallions), chopped

100 g (3½ oz) button mushrooms, chopped

2 teaspoons butter

2 teaspoons plain (all-purpose) flour

½ cup (125 ml) milk, plus extra for brushing

⅓ cup (50 g) mixed frozen peas and corn, thawed slightly

½ sheet frozen puff pastry

1 Preheat the oven to 200°C (400°F/Gas 6). Heat the oil in a non-stick frying pan over medium–high heat. Fry the chicken, stirring often, for 5 minutes, until brown and cooked. Place in a large bowl.

2 Reduce the heat to medium and fry the bacon, onion and mushrooms for 3 minutes, stirring often, until the bacon is cooked and the vegetables have softened. Add to the chicken.

3 Melt the butter in the frying pan, then add the flour. Cook, stirring, for about 30 seconds. Add the milk gradually, stirring constantly. Bring to a boil and cook for 1 minute, or until thickened.

4 Add the sauce to the chicken mixture, along with the peas and corn. Season to taste with salt and freshly ground black pepper and mix well.

5 Spoon into one or two 1 cup (250 ml) ramekin or ramekins and set on a baking tray. Cover with the pastry, pressing it down around the side of each ramekin. Brush lightly with milk and bake for 15–20 minutes, or until golden. Serve hot.

Each serving provides
2513 kJ, 600 kcal, 54 g protein, 32 g fat (14 g saturated fat), 24 g carbohydrate (5 g sugars), 3 g fibre, 1012 mg sodium

Cook's tip

Frozen pastry usually comes in sheets about 25 cm (10 inches) square. A ramekin that is about 10 cm (4 inches) across the top requires a square quarter from the pastry sheet. Take the pastry from the freezer and let it soften until it is just pliable enough to cut, but not completely thawed. Wrap the remainder in plastic and return to the freezer.

Other ideas

Stir-fries are very versatile — you can exchange ingredients to suit your taste, or ingredients you have on hand, and vary the flavour by adding spices such as chilli or ginger.

There are also many different stir-fry sauces in the supermarket to try; once opened, they will keep in the fridge for several weeks.

Stir-fry tips

■ Before you start cooking, measure out and chop all your ingredients as you won't have time to do this once you start stir-frying.

■ Cut foods to a uniform size, so they cook at the same rate.

■ Heat the wok or pan to the required temperature before adding food, as it needs to sear and begin to cook immediately. If the wok or pan is not hot enough, the food will stew rather than sizzle.

Chicken and vegetable stir-fry

Preparation 15 minutes

- -

Cooking 15 minutes

For 1

⅓ cup (65 g) jasmine rice
(Thai fragrant rice)

1 tablespoon soy sauce

2 teaspoons honey

2 teaspoons lime juice

150 g (5 oz) skinless, boneless
chicken thighs, trimmed

3 teaspoons vegetable oil

½ small carrot, thinly sliced
diagonally

60 g (2 oz) broccoli florets, halved
or quartered

50 g (1¾ oz) snow peas
(mangetout), halved diagonally

1 small clove garlic, crushed

1 spring onion (scallion), sliced
diagonally

For 2

⅔ cup (150 g) jasmine rice
(Thai fragrant rice)

2 tablespoons soy sauce

1 tablespoon honey

1 tablespoon lime juice

300 g (10 oz) skinless, boneless
chicken thighs, trimmed

1 tablespoon vegetable oil

1 small carrot, thinly sliced
diagonally

125 g (4 oz) broccoli florets,
halved or quartered

100 g (3½ oz) snow peas
(mangetout), halved diagonally

1 clove garlic, crushed

2 spring onions (scallions), sliced
diagonally

1 Bring a medium saucepan of water to a boil. Add the rice, stir once and return to a boil. Cook, uncovered, for 12 minutes, or until tender. Drain.

2 Meanwhile, combine the soy sauce, honey and lime juice and set aside. Cut each chicken thigh in half, then across the grain into thin strips.

3 Heat half the oil in a wok or deep frying pan over high heat. Stir-fry the chicken (in two batches, if cooking for two) for 2–3 minutes, or until golden and cooked through. Transfer to a plate.

4 Heat the remaining oil over medium–high heat. Stir-fry the carrot, broccoli and snow peas for 3 minutes, or until tender but still crisp. Add the garlic and spring onion and stir-fry for 30 seconds.

5 Add the chicken and soy sauce mixture. Stir-fry briefly just to heat through. Serve with the rice.

- -

Each serving provides
2603 kJ, 622 kcal, 38 g protein, 17 g fat (3 g saturated fat), 77 g carbohydrate (16 g sugars), 6 g fibre, 860 mg sodium

Spiced spatchcock

Preparation 20 minutes

Cooking 40 minutes

For 1

1 red-skinned potato, about 150 g
   (5 oz), washed

3 teaspoons olive oil

2 teaspoons lemon or lime juice

¼ teaspoon dried red chilli flakes

¼ teaspoon dried oregano

¼ teaspoon smoked paprika

a pinch of salt

1 small chicken, about 500 g
   (1 lb)

For 2

2 red-skinned potatoes, about
   150 g (5 oz) each, washed

1½ tablespoons olive oil

1 tablespoon lemon or lime juice

½ teaspoon dried red chilli flakes

½ teaspoon dried oregano

½ teaspoon smoked paprika

a pinch of salt

2 small chickens, about 500 g
   (1 lb) each

Each serving provides
2994 kJ, 715 kcal, 47 g protein, 50 g fat
(13 g saturated fat), 17 g carbohydrate
(1 g sugars), 2 g fibre, 499 mg sodium

Step 1 Preheat the oven to 200°C (400°F/ Gas 6). Cut each potato lengthwise into 8 wedges. Place in a large baking dish lined with baking paper, drizzle with half the oil and toss to coat. Start baking the potatoes while preparing the spatchcock. Mix the lemon or lime juice, spices, salt and remaining oil in a small bowl. Using kitchen scissors, cut down along each side of each bird's backbone, then pull out and discard the backbone.

Step 2 Open out the bird and place it on a board, cut side down. Press in the centre with the heel of your hand, to flatten the bird out.

<u>Step 3</u> Rub the spice mixture all over it, then add to the baking dish with the potatoes. Roast for 30 minutes, or until the potatoes are golden brown and the chicken juices run clear when the thickest part of the thigh is pierced with a skewer. Serve with your favourite steamed greens.

Quick ideas for... steak

Steaks are a perfectly portioned serving for one or two. Great steaks for pan-frying include fillet, minute, rump, rib-eye and sirloin. Serve with our luscious sauces or butters, mashed potato or crusty bread.

6 steps to a super steak

1 Take the meat out of the fridge about 20 minutes before cooking. This stops the pan temperature dropping when you add the meat, ensuring the steak sears immediately and caramelises on the surface, rather than stewing and becoming grey and unpleasant.

2 Preheat the frying pan to medium–high. Having a hot pan helps seal the meat quickly, so it doesn't stew. Heavy-based pans are best as they retain the heat. (If you are cooking a thick steak, sear it over high heat, then reduce the heat slightly and let it cook through to your liking.)

3 Oil the meat, rather than the pan. Excess oil in the pan will only burn and smoke over high heat.

4 Only turn the steak once during cooking. The cooking time will vary, depending on how thick it is. For a steak 2–3 cm (¾–1¼ inches) thick: cook for 2–3 minutes each side for rare; 4–5 minutes each side for medium; 5–6 minutes each side for well done. (If cooking a thick steak, sear it over high heat, then reduce the heat slightly and let it cook through to your liking so the outside doesn't blacken too much.)

5 Test for doneness. Gently press the steak with tongs. If it yields to pressure, it is rare or medium–rare; the firmer it feels, the more well done it is.

6 Rest before serving. Transfer the steak to a warm plate, cover loosely with foil and leave for about 5 minutes. This allows the meat to 'rest' and reabsorb the juices, for a tender result.

Perfect pan sauces

Resting your steak also gives you a chance to turn the lovely pan juices — or even just the browned bits on the bottom of the pan — into a fabulous sauce. You can simply add a good glug of red or white wine to the pan and stir over the heat to mix it with the pan juices (this is called 'deglazing'); at this point you can also add some mustard or chopped fresh herbs. Simmer for a minute or so, until reduced slightly, then drizzle over the steak. Alternatively, while the steak is resting, whip up one of the following sauces, which all serve 2. Halve the recipes to serve 1.

Steak diane

Melt 2 teaspoons **butter** in the frying pan over medium heat. Add 1 finely chopped **French shallot** and 1 crushed **garlic** clove and cook for 1 minute. Stir in 3 teaspoons **worcestershire sauce** and 2 teaspoons **brandy**, scraping the pan with a wooden spoon, then stir in 1/3 cup (80 ml) pouring (light) **cream**. Bring to a simmer and cook for 3 minutes, or until thickened slightly.

Mushroom marsala sauce

Melt 1 tablespoon **butter** in the frying pan over medium heat. Add 150 g (5 oz) sliced **button mushrooms** and sauté for 5 minutes, or until tender and lightly browned. Stir in 1 tablespoon **marsala** and 1/3 cup (80 ml) pouring (light) **cream**. Simmer for 3–4 minutes, or until thickened slightly.

Red wine sauce

Melt 1 tablespoon **butter** in the frying pan over medium heat. Add 1/2 small finely sliced **onion** and cook for 5 minutes, or until soft and golden. Add 1 tablespoon **redcurrant jelly**, 1/4 cup (60 ml) **red wine** and 1 1/4 cups (310 ml) **beef stock**. Bring to a simmer and cook for 5 minutes, or until reduced slightly. Return the steak to the pan, then turn to coat in the sauce and gently reheat.

Gravy

Melt 2 teaspoons **butter** in the frying pan. Sprinkle in 2 teaspoons plain (all-purpose) **flour** and cook over medium heat for 30 seconds, scraping the bottom of the pan. Stir in 1/2 cup (125 ml) **beef stock**, a little at a time, stirring well until smooth. Bring to a simmer and cook for 1 minute, or until thickened.

Quick creamy sauces

Add one of the following ingredients to the pan: 2 teaspoons mustard; 1/2 teaspoon freshly ground black pepper; 1 teaspoon finely grated lemon zest; or 1 teaspoon chopped fresh rosemary; then stir in 1/3 cup (80 ml) pouring (light) cream and simmer for 1–2 minutes.

Flavoured butters

To jazz up a plain steak, soften 60 g (2 oz) butter to room temperature, then mix in any of the following: 1 tablespoon mustard; 1 tablespoon chopped fresh herbs, such as parsley, thyme, rosemary, dill or chives (or a mixture); 1 teaspoon finely grated lemon zest; 1 crushed garlic clove; 1 teaspoon finely chopped fresh red chilli; 1 mashed anchovy; or 1 teaspoon finely chopped capers.

You can also combine flavours — try garlic, lemon and chilli; or anchovy, capers and dill. Another tasty idea is to combine equal parts soft blue cheese and butter.

Hot to use Chill the flavoured butter until firm, then divide it into 6 serving portions. Place the excess portions in a zip-lock bag, expel the air and freeze for up to 1 month. Serve each portion over a warm steak.

Another idea

To make Yorkshire puddings (for two), combine ½ cup (75 g) plain (all-purpose) flour and a good pinch of salt in a bowl. Make a well in the centre. Whisk ½ cup (125 ml) milk and 1 egg together, then whisk into the flour until smooth. Pour the batter into a jug and rest for 20 minutes.

Just before you are ready to cook, place ½ teaspoon vegetable oil into each of four ⅓ cup (80 ml) muffin holes and place in the oven for 5 minutes to heat. Quickly divide the batter among the four muffin holes and return the tray to the top shelf of the oven. Cook for 15 minutes, or until puffed and golden brown.

Roast beef dinner

Preparation 20 minutes

Cooking 40 minutes

For 2

2 potatoes, peeled

olive oil spray

1 small onion, cut into 6 wedges

1 tablespoon butter

1 beef fillet steak, 2 cm (1 inch) thick, and weighing about 300 g (10 oz)

2 teaspoons plain (all-purpose) flour

½ cup (125 ml) beef stock

Each serving provides
1483 kJ, 354 kcal, 31 g protein, 17 g fat (8 g saturated fat), 18 g carbohydrate (2 g sugars), 2 g fibre, 385 mg sodium

1 Preheat the oven to 200°C (400°F/Gas 6). Cut each potato into quarters and place in a small saucepan. Cover with cold water, bring to a boil over medium heat, then cook for 5 minutes, or until just tender. Drain well, then shake the pan to rough up the potato.

2 Place the potato in a shallow baking dish, spray with olive oil and roast for 15 minutes. Add the onion, spray with a little oil, then roast for a further 10 minutes, or until the vegetables are golden brown.

3 Meanwhile, melt half the butter in a frying pan over high heat. Sear the beef all over until well browned. Reserving the frying pan and pan juices, add the beef to the baking dish with the vegetables for the last 6 minutes of roasting. Remove the beef from the oven and leave to rest for 5 minutes before slicing into 4–6 slices.

4 Melt the remaining butter in the reserved frying pan. Sprinkle the flour over and cook, stirring, for about 30 seconds. Add the stock, a little at a time, stirring well between each addition, until smooth. Bring to a boil and cook for 1 minute, or until thickened slightly.

5 Serve the sauce over the meat and vegetables, with Yorkshire puddings if desired.

Serving suggestions

Simply serve with steamed brussels sprouts or green beans. For a more substantial meal, serve with Yorkshire puddings, see page 150.

Sausage and bean hotpot

For 2

Preparation 10 minutes
- -
Cooking 25 minutes

2 teaspoons olive oil

4 thin beef sausages

½ small onion, chopped

100 g (3½ oz) button mushrooms, sliced

1 small clove garlic, crushed

410 g (15 oz) can chopped tomatoes

¼ cup (60 ml) beef stock

400 g (14 oz) can cannellini beans, rinsed and drained

2 tablespoons chopped fresh parsley

a pinch of brown sugar

crusty bread, to serve

- -

Each serving provides
2313 kJ, 553 kcal, 27 g protein, 36 g fat
(15 g saturated fat), 32 g carbohydrate
(8 g sugars), 16 g fibre, 1158 mg sodium

1 Heat half the oil in a large deep frying pan over medium–high heat. Brown the sausages, turning occasionally, for 5 minutes. Transfer to a board, cool slightly, then thickly slice.

2 Heat the remaining oil in the pan over medium heat and cook the onion for 3 minutes, or until soft. Add the mushrooms and cook for a further 2 minutes, or until soft. Add the garlic and cook for 1 minute.

3 Stir in the tomatoes, stock and sausages. Bring to a boil, then reduce the heat slightly. Simmer, partially covered, for 15 minutes, or until the sausages are cooked through.

4 Stir in the beans, parsley and sugar. Season with salt and freshly ground black pepper and serve with crusty bread.

Other ideas

■ Use canned brown lentils instead of beans.

■ Add some chopped chilli if you like a bit of heat.

■ Omit the sausages and increase the beans (or include a mixture). Use vegetable stock instead of beef stock.

It is worth making this for two people, as it freezes well in an airtight container, once cooled completely. Leftovers will also keep for a few days in the fridge for another meal. Try it with wholegrain toast as a warming winter breakfast.

This stew is fabulous with mashed potato. It needs long simmering, so make it in bulk, then freeze leftovers for other snappy meals. The variations use 2 serves of stew; halve them to serve 1.

Beef stew

Makes **8 serves**

Preparation **20 minutes**

Cooking **2½ hours**

2 tablespoons vegetable oil

1.5 kg (3 lb) stewing beef, cut into 3 cm (1¼ inch) cubes

1 large onion, chopped

2 tablespoons plain (all-purpose) flour

1½ cups (375 ml) beef stock

410 g (15 oz) can chopped tomatoes

2 carrots, halved and sliced

Instead of finishing the stew on the stove in step 3, you can transfer it to a covered ovenproof dish and cook in a preheated 150ºC (300ºF/Gas 2) oven for 2 hours.

1 Heat half the oil in a heavy-based saucepan over high heat. Brown the beef in four batches, stirring often; the meat will at first stick to the pan, until it begins to sear, so add a little more oil between batches if necessary. Set the beef aside.

2 Reduce the heat to medium and heat the rest of the oil. Fry the onion for 5 minutes, or until soft and golden. Sprinkle the flour over and stir for 30 seconds. Gradually stir in the stock, scraping the base of the pan to stop lumps forming.

3 Stir in the tomatoes and add the beef. Cover and bring to a boil, then reduce the heat as low as possible, so the liquid is only just simmering. Cook, covered, for 1 hour, stirring occasionally.

4 Add the carrots, cover and cook for 45 minutes, stirring occasionally. Remove the lid and cook, uncovered, a further 10 minutes, or until thickened and reduced slightly — you'll need to increase the heat a little to keep the liquid at a simmer. Season with salt and freshly ground black pepper.

5 To freeze, cool completely, then divide into portions for 1 or 2 and place in airtight containers or zip-lock bags. Label, date and freeze for up to 3 months. To use, thaw in the microwave, or overnight in the fridge.

Ways to use beef stew

Beef pies

Preheat the oven to 200°C (400°F/Gas 6) and grease two 1 cup (250 ml) pie dishes. Thaw 1 sheet of frozen **shortcrust pastry** and cut into quarters. Line each pie dish with a square of shortcrust pastry, then fill with the room-temperature **beef stew**. Top with another pastry square, then trim the edges and press together to seal. Brush with a little **beaten egg** if you like. Bake for 25 minutes, or until golden brown.

Beef curry

Heat 1 teaspoon **oil** in a deep frying pan over medium–low heat. Add 2 crushed **garlic** cloves and 3 teaspoons **curry powder** and stir for 1 minute. Add the **beef stew**, 1¾ cups (80 g) **baby English spinach leaves** and ⅓ cup (80 ml) **coconut milk** and stir to combine. Bring to a boil over medium heat, then reduce the heat and simmer for 2 minutes. Sprinkle with chopped **coriander (cilantro)** and serve with **steamed rice**.

Tagine with couscous

Heat 1 teaspoon **olive oil** in a deep frying pan over medium–low heat. Add 2 crushed **garlic** cloves, 1½ teaspoons finely grated **fresh ginger** and 1½ teaspoons **Moroccan seasoning**. Cook, stirring, for 1 minute. Add the **beef stew** and ⅓ cup (55 g) chopped **pitted dates**. Bring to a boil over medium heat, then reduce the heat and simmer for 2 minutes. Sprinkle with chopped **parsley** and serve with **couscous**.

Ragu with pasta

Heat 1 teaspoon **oil** in a deep frying pan over medium–low heat. Add 1 crushed **garlic** clove and 2 tablespoons **tomato paste** (concentrated purée). Cook, stirring, for 1 minute. Add the **beef stew** and 1 teaspoon **dried Italian herbs**. Bring to a boil over medium heat and simmer for 2 minutes. Serve over cooked **short pasta** such as penne or fusili, topped with grated **parmesan**.

Stroganoff-style beef with noodles

Heat 2 teaspoons **olive oil** in a deep frying pan over medium–low heat. Add 100 g (3½ oz) sliced **button mushrooms**, 1 crushed **garlic** clove and 1 teaspoon **paprika**. Cook, stirring, for 2 minutes. Add the **beef stew** and bring to a boil over medium heat, then reduce the heat and simmer for 2 minutes. Stir in ⅓ cup (80 ml) pouring (light) **cream** and heat through. Sprinkle with chopped **parsley** and serve with cooked **tagliatelle**, or other wide, flat noodles.

Stewing secrets

- Inexpensive cuts such as chuck steak and gravy beef are great for stewing, as they become 'fall-apart' tender and delicious.

- When browning the meat, make sure the heat is high and the beef is added in small batches, so the pan temperature remains high and the meat browns. You don't need to cook the meat through at this point — just brown the surfaces to develop a rich flavour.

- The flour thickens the gravy. Make sure you 'cook' it a little before adding the stock, to remove the raw flour taste.

- During the long simmering stage, make sure the heat is very low so the meat doesn't toughen, and keep the pan covered to keep the juices in.

Classic hamburger

Preparation 15 minutes

Cooking 15 minutes

Quick

For 1

½ small onion

125 g (4 oz) lean minced (ground) beef

2 teaspoons tomato paste (concentrated purée)

2 teaspoons olive oil

1 slice cheddar

1 egg

1 large iceberg lettuce leaf, torn

1 wholemeal (whole-wheat) bread roll, split and toasted

2 slices tomato

tomato sauce (ketchup) or barbecue sauce, to serve

For 2

1 small onion

250 g (8 oz) lean minced (ground) beef

1 tablespoon tomato paste (concentrated purée)

2 teaspoons olive oil

2 slices cheddar

2 eggs

2 large iceberg lettuce leaves, torn

2 wholemeal (whole-wheat) bread rolls, split and toasted

4 slices tomato

tomato sauce (ketchup) or barbecue sauce, to serve

1 Finely chop half the onion; place in a bowl with the beef and tomato paste. Season with salt and freshly ground black pepper and mix well. Shape into one or two flat patties, about 12 cm (4½ inches) across — the meat will shrink during cooking.

2 Heat the oil in a non-stick frying pan over medium–low heat. Slice the remaining onion and cook for 5 minutes, or until soft and golden. Transfer to a plate.

3 Cook the patty or patties in the pan over medium heat for about 4 minutes. Turn and cook for 2 minutes, then place a cheese slice on each patty and cook for a further 2 minutes.

4 Break the egg or eggs into the pan and cook for 2 minutes, or until the white has set but the yolk is still soft. (Alternatively, cook to your liking.)

5 Arrange the lettuce on the base of each roll, then top with a patty. Top with the fried onion, tomato slices and an egg, then drizzle with tomato or barbecue sauce. Replace the top of the roll or rolls and serve immediately.

Each serving provides
2340 kJ, 559 kcal, 43 g protein, 31 g fat (11 g saturated fat), 26 g carbohydrate (4 g sugars), 4 g fibre, 633 mg sodium

Thai beef red curry

Preparation 15 minutes

Cooking 10 minutes

For 2

250 g (8 oz) rump steak

3 teaspoons vegetable oil

½ small onion, sliced lengthwise

½ small red capsicum (bell pepper), cut into long strips

60 g (2 oz) snow peas (mangetout), trimmed, then halved lengthwise on the diagonal

½ head broccoli, about 180 g (6 oz), trimmed and cut into small florets

1 tablespoon Thai red curry paste

½ cup (125 ml) coconut milk

2 teaspoons fish sauce

juice of ½ lime

1 teaspoon brown sugar

4–5 sprigs coriander (cilantro), to garnish

steamed jasmine rice (Thai fragrant rice), to serve

Each serving provides
1759 kJ, 420 kcal, 35 g protein, 27 g fat
(15 g saturated fat), 9 g carbohydrate
(7 g sugars), 6 g fibre, 553 mg sodium

Step 1 Cut the steak into very thin slices across the grain. Heat 1 teaspoon of the oil in a wok or large deep non-stick frying pan over medium–high heat. Stir-fry half the meat and half the onion for 2 minutes, until just browned; remove to a plate. Heat another 1 teaspoon oil in the pan, stir-fry the remaining beef and onion, then remove to the plate.

Step 2 Heat the remaining oil, then stir-fry the capsicum, snow peas and broccoli for 2 minutes. Add the curry paste and stir-fry for 1 minute. Add the meat and onion, then pour in the coconut milk. Bring to a boil, reduce the heat and simmer for 2 minutes.

Thai red curry paste is sold in jars or cans in most large supermarkets. Once opened, it will keep for several weeks in the fridge.

Step 3 Stir in the fish sauce, lime juice and sugar. Top with coriander leaves and serve with steamed jasmine rice.

Many meals from one bolognese sauce

Cook up and freeze a big batch of this classic sauce for easy meals.
Use it in the recipes here, or over pasta with grated parmesan. Most
variation recipes use two bolognese portions; halve them to serve 1.

Basic bolognese

Makes 8 serves

Preparation 20 minutes

Cooking 1½ hours

2 tablespoons olive oil

2 onions, finely chopped

3 celery stalks, finely chopped

2 carrots, grated

3 cloves garlic, crushed

500 g (1 lb) minced (ground) beef

500 g (1 lb) minced (ground) pork

1½ cups (375 ml) beef stock

2 x 410 g (15 oz) cans chopped tomatoes

¼ cup (60 g) tomato paste (concentrated purée)

1 teaspoon dried oregano

1 Heat the oil in a large heavy-based saucepan over medium–low heat. Add the onions, celery, carrots and garlic and cook for 10 minutes, stirring often, until soft and lightly golden. Add the beef and pork and cook until browned, breaking up any lumps with a wooden spoon.

2 Stir in the stock, tomatoes, tomato paste and oregano. Bring to a boil, then reduce the heat and simmer, partially covered, for 1 hour.

3 Check the liquid: if the sauce looks too soupy, remove the lid and cook for a further 10 minutes, until reduced and thickened slightly. Season with salt and freshly ground black pepper.

4 To freeze, cool completely, then divide into portions for 1 or 2 and place in airtight containers or zip-lock bags. Label, date and freeze for up to 3 months. To use, thaw in the microwave, or overnight in the fridge.

Long, slow cooking gives the bolognese a rich flavour and melt-in-the-mouth texture. You can cook it for a shorter time if you wish.

Ways to use bolognese

Chilli con carne or tacos

Heat 1 teaspoon **oil** in a deep frying pan over medium–low heat. Add 1 crushed **garlic** clove, 1 teaspoon **ground cumin** and ½ teaspoon **chilli powder**. Cook, stirring, for 30 seconds. Add the **bolognese** mixture, two 125 g (4 oz) cans rinsed, drained **red kidney beans** and a 125 g (4 oz) can drained **corn kernels**. Bring to a boil over medium heat and simmer for 2 minutes. Serve either with **corn chips** or **tortillas** and a dollop of **sour cream**, or in warmed **taco shells** with shredded **lettuce**, chopped **tomatoes** and grated **cheese**.

Individual cottage pies

Preheat a grill (broiler) to high. Peel 500 g (1 lb) **potatoes**, chop into 2 cm (¾ inch) chunks, place in a saucepan and cover with **water**. Bring to a boil and cook for 10 minutes, or until tender. Drain and mash, then mix in 1 tablespoon **butter** and ¼ cup (60 ml) **milk**. Season with **salt** and freshly ground **black pepper**.

Meanwhile, heat the **bolognese** in a saucepan. Add 1 tablespoon **gravy powder**, 2 teaspoons **worcestershire sauce** and ⅓ cup (50 g) frozen **peas**. Spoon the bolognese into two 1 cup (250 ml) ramekins and top with the mashed potato. Grill (broil) for 8 minutes, or until golden brown on top.

Beef moussaka

Preheat the oven to 180°C (350°F/Gas 4). Arrange a layer of **chargrilled eggplant (aubergine)** slices in a 4 cup (1 litre) baking dish that measures about 20 x 15 x 5 cm (8 x 6 x 2 inches). Spread with half the **bolognese**. Top with another eggplant layer, then the remaining bolognese. Melt 1½ tablespoons **butter** in a small saucepan over low heat. Add 1 tablespoon **plain (all-purpose) flour** and cook, stirring, for 1 minute. Gradually add 1 cup (250 ml) **milk**, stirring constantly until smooth. Add a tiny pinch of grated **nutmeg** and season with **salt**. Spread the sauce over the bolognese and sprinkle with ½ cup (60 g) grated **cheddar**. Bake for 15 minutes, until golden.

Cook's tip You can buy chargrilled eggplant — you'll need about 25 g (8 oz). Alternatively, slice 1 large eggplant, brush with oil and chargrill or pan-fry until tender and lightly browned.

Easy lasagne

Preheat the oven to 200°C (400°F/Gas 6). Grease a 4 cup (1 litre) baking dish that measures about 20 x 15 x 5 cm (8 x 6 x 2 inches). Arrange a layer of **instant lasagne sheets** (no-cook lasagne noodles) in the dish, trimming to fit. (You'll need a 250 g/8 oz packet of lasagne.) Spread with half the **bolognese**, then add another layer of lasagne sheets. In a bowl, mash 150 g (5 oz) **fresh ricotta** and 1 cup (45 g) shredded **baby English spinach leaves** until combined; add a pinch of grated **nutmeg**, season to taste, then spread over the lasagne. Add another layer of lasagne sheets, the remaining bolognese, then a final layer of lasagne. Cover with ¾ cup (180 ml) **tomato pasta sauce**, then a sheet of lightly oiled foil. Bake for 30 minutes, then discard the foil. Sprinkle with ½ cup (75 g) grated **mozzarella** and bake for a further 15 minutes, or until golden brown.

Beef and rice in lettuce cups

Cook ⅓ cup (65 g) **long-grain rice** in a saucepan of boiling water for 10 minutes, or until tender. Drain well. Heat a single portion of **bolognese** in a saucepan or in the microwave, then combine it with the rice. Allow to cool slightly, then stir in 1 tablespoon **sweet chilli sauce** and 2 teaspoons **soy sauce**. Serve in **iceberg lettuce** cups.

Cook's tips

Nick the edges of the meat with a sharp
knife to stop it curling during cooking.

If your escalope is more than 5 mm
(¼ inch) thick, or of an uneven thickness,
beat it with a meat mallet or rolling pin
to make it thinner and more even.

Veal escalopes with sage and lemon

Preparation 10 minutes

Cooking 15 minutes

Quick

One-pot

For 1

3 teaspoons olive oil

¼ small onion, chopped

1 small zucchini (courgette), diced

1 small clove garlic, crushed

125 g (4 oz) cherry tomatoes, halved

1 cup (45 g) baby English spinach leaves

1 veal escalope, about 150 g (5 oz), cut in half

2 large fresh sage leaves, shredded

1 tablespoon lemon juice

crusty bread, to serve

For 2

1 tablespoon olive oil

½ small onion, chopped

1 zucchini (courgette), diced

1 clove garlic, crushed

250 g (8 oz) cherry tomatoes, halved

2 cups (90 g) baby English spinach leaves

2 veal escalopes, about 150 g (5 oz) each, cut in half

4 large fresh sage leaves, shredded

2 tablespoons lemon juice

crusty bread, to serve

1 Heat half the oil in a non-stick frying pan over medium heat. Fry the onion for 3–4 minutes, or until soft. Add the zucchini and garlic and cook, stirring often, for 3–4 minutes, or until tender.

2 Add the tomatoes and spinach. Cook, stirring often, for 5 minutes, or until the tomatoes have softened slightly and the spinach has wilted. Season to taste with salt and freshly ground black pepper, then transfer to a serving plate or plates and set aside in a warm place.

3 Wipe out the pan and heat the remaining oil over high heat. Cook the veal for 1 minute on each side, or until browned and cooked through. Transfer to a serving plate or plates.

4 Reduce the heat to medium and add the sage to the pan. Cook, stirring, for 30 seconds, then stir the lemon juice into the pan juices. Pour the juices over the veal and serve with crusty bread.

Other ideas

You can also use thin pieces of beef or pork, or horizontally cut a skinless chicken breast in half and beat to an even thickness. Thin cuts are handy to have in the freezer as they thaw quickly.

Each serving provides
1171 kJ, 280 kcal, 37 g protein, 12 g fat (2 g saturated fat), 5 g carbohydrate (5 g sugars), 4 g fibre, 99 mg sodium

Pan-fried pork chops

Preparation 15 minutes

Cooking 15 minutes

For 1

2 small new potatoes, about 50 g
   (1³/₄ oz) each, halved

1 teaspoon vegetable oil

1 pork cutlet, about 160 g (5¹/₂ oz)

1 teaspoon butter

1 small green apple, peeled, cored
   and thinly sliced

³/₄ cup (55 g) finely shredded red
   cabbage

a small pinch of caraway seeds

¹/₄ teaspoon brown sugar

¹/₄ teaspoon red wine vinegar

1 tablespoon chopped fresh
   parsley or herb of your choice

For 2

4 small new potatoes, about 50 g
   (1³/₄ oz) each, halved

2 teaspoons vegetable oil

2 pork cutlets, about 160 g
   (5¹/₂ oz) each

2 teaspoons butter

1 green apple, peeled, cored and
   thinly sliced

1¹/₂ cups (115 g) finely shredded
   red cabbage

a pinch of caraway seeds

¹/₂ teaspoon brown sugar

¹/₂ teaspoon red wine vinegar

2 tablespoons chopped fresh
   parsley or herb of your choice

1 Place the potatoes in a medium saucepan and cover with water. Put the lid on and bring to a boil over medium–high heat, then tilt the lid and cook for about 10 minutes, or until the potatoes are tender.

2 Meanwhile, heat the oil in a non-stick frying pan over medium heat. Add the pork and cook for 4 minutes on each side, or until browned and cooked through. Set aside on a warm plate or plates and cover loosely with foil.

3 Melt half the butter in the same frying pan. Add the apple slices and cook for 2 minutes, turning once, then add the cabbage and caraway

seeds. Cook, stirring, for 5 minutes, or until the cabbage is soft. Stir in the sugar and vinegar, then season to taste with salt and freshly ground black pepper.

4 Drain the potatoes and toss with the remaining butter and the parsley. Season to taste. Serve with the pork and sautéed cabbage.

Each serving provides
1638 kJ, 391 kcal, 37 g protein, 16 g fat (6 g saturated fat), 25 g carbohydrate (11 g sugars), 6 g fibre, 155 mg sodium

Other ideas

■ When the weather is cooler, serve the pork with mashed potato, steamed green vegetables and a dollop of cranberry sauce or redcurrant jelly.

■ Replace the apple with pear.

Cook's tips

■ Leftover cannellini beans can be frozen. Place in a zip-lock bag, expel the excess air and seal tightly.

■ Make fresh breadcrumbs by processing leftover bread in a food processor until coarse crumbs form. Keep in a zip-lock bag in the freezer and use up as needed.

Pork patty with tomato and bean salad

Preparation 20 minutes

Cooking 10 minutes

For 1

100 g (3½ oz) minced (ground) pork

¼ cup (20 g) fresh breadcrumbs

½ green apple, grated

½ teaspoon dried sage

2 spring onions (scallions), chopped

3 teaspoons olive oil

½ a 400 g (14 oz) can cannellini beans, rinsed and drained

60 g (2 oz) cherry tomatoes, halved

½ cup (20 g) baby English spinach leaves

¼ small avocado, diced

1 teaspoon red wine vinegar

For 2

200 g (7 oz) minced (ground) pork

½ cup (40 g) fresh breadcrumbs

1 small green apple, grated

1 teaspoon dried sage

4 spring onions (scallions), chopped

1 tablespoon olive oil

400 g (14 oz) can cannellini beans, rinsed and drained

125 g (4 oz) cherry tomatoes, halved

1 cup (45 g) baby English spinach leaves

½ small avocado, diced

2 teaspoons red wine vinegar

1 Place the pork in a bowl with the breadcrumbs, apple, sage and half the spring onion. Season with salt and freshly ground black pepper and mix well. Shape into one or two flat patties, about 12 cm (4½ inches) across — the meat will shrink during cooking.

2 Heat 1 teaspoon of the oil in a non-stick frying pan over medium heat. Cook the patty or patties for 4 minutes on each side, or until browned and cooked through.

3 Meanwhile, combine the beans, tomatoes, spinach, avocado and remaining spring onion in a bowl. Drizzle with the vinegar and remaining oil and season to taste.

4 Lightly toss the salad and serve with the pork.

Each serving provides
2435 kJ, 582 kcal, 36 g protein, 29 g fat (6 g saturated fat), 44 g carbohydrate (10 g sugars), 14 g fibre, 324 mg sodium

Pork with creamy garlic mustard sauce

Preparation 10 minutes

Cooking 10 minutes

For 1

1 teaspoon vegetable oil

1 pork butterfly steak, about 200 g (7 oz)

1 teaspoon butter

1 small clove garlic, thinly sliced

2 teaspoons medium-dry sherry

1 teaspoon wholegrain mustard

¼ cup (60 ml) pouring cream

For 2

2 teaspoons vegetable oil

2 pork butterfly steaks, about 200 g (7 oz) each

2 teaspoons butter

1 clove garlic, thinly sliced

1 tablespoon medium-dry sherry

2 teaspoons wholegrain mustard

½ cup (125 ml) pouring cream

1 Heat the oil in a frying pan over medium–high heat. Cook the pork for 3 minutes on each side, or until browned and tender. Set aside on a warm serving plate or plates and cover loosely with foil.

2 Reduce the heat to medium–low and add the butter and garlic to the pan. Cook, stirring, for 30 seconds, or until the garlic is just soft — don't let it become too brown or it will turn bitter.

3 Stir in the sherry, mustard and cream. Bring to a boil, then simmer for 2 minutes to thicken slightly. Drizzle over the pork and serve.

Serving suggestions

Lovely with steamed green vegetables and carrots, or wilt some shredded baby English spinach in the creamy sauce.

Other ideas

- Try different cuts of pork with this sauce.
- Instead of pork, use beef or chicken.
- Use reduced-fat cream if you want to make this dish a little lighter.

Each serving provides
2303 kJ, 550 kcal, 44 g protein, 39 g fat (22 g saturated fat), 2 g carbohydrate (2 g sugars), <1 g fibre, 163 mg sodium

lamb cutlets

Simple to prepare, and so quick to cook, lamb cutlets make a delectable, perfectly portioned meal. This lovely little cut of meat lends itself to a world of flavours. Allow three cutlets per person.

3 steps to perfect lamb cutlets

1 Preheat the pan or barbecue Preheat the grill (broiler), barbecue, frying pan or chargrill pan so it is hot before adding the cutlets. Brush each cutlet lightly with olive oil or vegetable oil and season as desired.

2 Turn once only Cook the cutlets on one side until the first sign of moisture appears on top. Turn and cook for 2–3 minutes, or until done as desired. Only turn once, for a tender result.

3 Rest before serving Like other meats, lamb cutlets benefit from a brief resting. To ensure they are tender, remove the cutlets from heat, transfer to a plate, loosely cover with foil, and stand for 5 minutes before serving.

Lean and healthy

If you want to cut down on fat, look for 'frenched' or 'French-trimmed' cutlets. These cutlets are already well trimmed of fat, and have the bone scraped clean for an elegant presentation.

Indian-style cutlets

Mix together some **natural (plain) yogurt**, a little crushed **garlic**, some finely grated **fresh ginger** and a pinch each of **ground cumin** and **ground turmeric**. Alternatively, mix some yogurt with a spoonful of your favourite **Indian curry paste**. Brush the mixture over the cutlets, avoiding the bone as much as possible, and leave to marinate if desired. Cook in a hot non-stick frying pan over medium–high heat for 2–3 minutes on each side, or until just pink in the middle. Serve with **steamed rice** and a **tomato**, **cucumber** and **mint** salad.

South-East Asian cutlets

Heat a frying pan or chargrill to medium–high. Brush the cutlets with **olive oil**, then cook for 2–3 minutes on each side, or until brown and tender. Serve drizzled with **Satay sauce** (see page 245), with some **iceberg lettuce**, **tomato** wedges, sliced **cucumber** and **steamed rice** or boiled **new potatoes**.

Greek-style cutlets

Marinate the cutlets in a little **lemon juice**, **olive oil** and crushed **garlic**, with some dried or chopped fresh **oregano**. Cook in a hot, non-stick frying pan over medium–high heat for 2–3 minutes on each side, or until just pink in the middle. Serve with a salad of **baby English spinach leaves**, halved **cherry tomatoes**, finely sliced **red onion** and canned **white beans**, dressed with **olive oil**.

Crumbed cutlets

Spread some **flour** and **breadcrumbs** on separate plates; lightly beat 1 **egg** in a shallow bowl. Dust the meat of each cutlet with the flour and shake off the excess. Brush the meat with the beaten egg, avoiding the bone, then gently press the breadcrumbs on. (At this point the cutlets can be placed on a plate in a single layer and refrigerated for 15 minutes, or even several hours, to help the crumbs adhere.) Heat about 1 cm (½ inch) **oil** in a frying pan over medium heat. Cook the cutlets for 2–3 minutes on each side, or until the crumbs are golden and the meat is just pink in the middle. Serve with mashed **potato**, steamed **green beans** and **carrots**, and a spoonful of **tomato chutney**.

Continental cutlets

Heat a frying pan or chargrill to medium–high. Brush the cutlets with **olive oil**, then cook for 2–3 minutes on each side, or until brown and tender. Rest for 5 minutes, then brush with **redcurrant jelly** and serve with buttered steamed **carrots**, and a mash of **potato**, **peas** and chopped **fresh mint**.

Middle Eastern cutlets 1

Heat a frying pan or chargrill to medium–high. Brush the cutlets with **olive oil**, then cook for 2–3 minutes on each side, or until brown and tender. Serve with a good spoonful of **hummus**, canned **baby beetroot** (beet), some **fetta** and **baby English spinach leaves** dressed with **lemon juice** and **olive oil**, and some warmed **pita bread**.

Middle Eastern cutlets 2

Heat a frying pan or chargrill to medium–high. Brush the cutlets with **olive oil** and 1 crushed **garlic** clove, then cook for 2–3 minutes on each side, or until brown and tender. Serve with a chickpea currant salad. To make a salad for two, soak 2 tablespoons **currants** in 1 tablespoon **lemon juice** for 10 minutes, then toss together with 2 teaspoons **olive oil**, 1 grated **carrot**, 2 finely sliced **spring onions** (scallions), 1 cup (185 g) drained canned **chickpeas** and about 4 tablespoons chopped **fresh parsley**.

Mini lamb roast with red wine gravy

For 2

Preparation 15 minutes

- -

Cooking 45 minutes

1 x 400 g (14 oz) boneless lamb
  mini roast (rump)

1½ tablespoons redcurrant jelly

1 clove garlic, sliced

1 sprig fresh rosemary, leaves
  picked

4 small new potatoes

1 onion, quartered

6 baby carrots, halved lengthwise
  if thick

2 small zucchini (courgettes),
  cut in half lengthwise

2 teaspoons olive oil

Red wine gravy

¼ cup (60 ml) red wine

½ cup (125 ml) chicken stock

2 teaspoons plain (all-purpose)
  flour

2 teaspoons softened butter

- -

Each serving provides
2616 kJ, 625 kcal, 50 g protein, 23 g fat
(8 g saturated fat), 49 g carbohydrate
(22 g sugars), 9 g fibre, 425 mg sodium

1 Preheat the oven to 200°C (400°F/Gas 6). Make several deep incisions in the lamb, using a small sharp knife. Brush the redcurrant jelly over the lamb, then push the garlic slices and rosemary leaves into the slits. Place the lamb in a roasting pan.

2 Place the vegetables in a bowl, drizzle with the oil and turn to coat all over. Season with salt and freshly ground black pepper, then arrange in the roasting pan, around the lamb. Roast for 35 minutes, or until the lamb is cooked but still slightly pink in the middle.

3 Remove the lamb to a warm plate and loosely cover with foil. Allow to rest in a warm place for 5–10 minutes to let the juices settle before carving. Meanwhile, roast the vegetables for a further 10 minutes, or until tender. Remove to a warm dish and keep warm.

4 To make the gravy, pour the roasting juices and sediment into a saucepan. Stir in the wine and stock over medium heat until any solid bits have dissolved, then bring to a boil. Combine the flour and butter well, then whisk into the pan juices. Reduce the heat to low and stir for several minutes, until the sauce thickens into a gravy. Season to taste.

5 Serve the lamb and vegetables with the gravy.

Other ideas

- Omit the redcurrant jelly, garlic and rosemary and instead brush the lamb with 3 teaspoons wholegrain mustard halfway through roasting.
- Roast other vegetables with the lamb, such as eggplant (aubergine), capsicum (bell pepper), fennel, parsnip, sweet potato and pumpkin (winter squash).
- Minted peas are also great with lamb.

Cook's tip

Here's another recipe that is best made for two people, even if dining solo. The leftover lamb can be used in so many ways — in a salad, on a gourmet sandwich or roll, or tossed through couscous or a Mediterranean-style pasta dish.

Instead of lamb, try thinly sliced beef or chicken, or even deveined raw prawns (shrimp).

Lamb and ginger stir-fry

Preparation 10 minutes

Cooking 6 minutes

For 1

1 teaspoon vegetable oil

100 g (3½ oz) lamb backstraps or loin fillets, thinly sliced

1 small clove garlic, crushed

½ teaspoon finely grated fresh ginger

½ small red capsicum (bell pepper), thinly sliced

2 spring onions (scallions), thinly sliced diagonally

5 snow peas (mangetout), trimmed and cut in half diagonally

2 teaspoons salt-reduced soy sauce

1 teaspoon honey

a few drops of sesame oil

½ teaspoon toasted sesame seeds

steamed rice, to serve

For 2

2 teaspoons vegetable oil

200 g (7 oz) lamb backstraps or loin fillets, thinly sliced

1 clove garlic, crushed

1 teaspoon finely grated fresh ginger

1 small red capsicum (bell pepper), thinly sliced

4 spring onions (scallions), thinly sliced diagonally

10 snow peas (mangetout), trimmed and cut in half diagonally

1 tablespoon salt-reduced soy sauce

2 teaspoons honey

a few drops of sesame oil

1 teaspoon toasted sesame seeds

steamed rice, to serve

1 Heat the oil in a wok or non-stick frying pan over high heat. Add the lamb and stir-fry for 2–3 minutes, or until sealed on both sides.

2 Add the garlic, ginger, capsicum, spring onions and snow peas. Toss quickly for about 2 minutes, to cook the vegetables evenly.

3 Add the soy sauce, honey and sesame oil, tossing well to coat the meat and vegetables.

4 Sprinkle with the sesame seeds and serve with steamed rice.

Leftover magic

■ Any leftover uncooked lamb can be wrapped tightly and frozen for up to a month. Thaw before using in another recipe.

■ Toasted sesame seeds can be refrigerated in an airtight container for up to 2 weeks.

Each serving provides
1132 kJ, 270 kcal, 24 g protein, 15 g fat (5 g saturated fat), 11 g carbohydrate (10 g sugars), 2 g fibre, 448 mg sodium

Greek-style lamb and salad

Preparation 15 minutes + 15 minutes marinating

Cooking 5 minutes

For 1

150 g (5 oz) lamb leg steaks

1 small clove garlic, crushed

½ teaspoon finely grated lemon zest

2 teaspoons lemon juice

½ teaspoon dried oregano

3 teaspoons olive oil

Greek-style salad

1 small tomato, cut into wedges

½ small red or green capsicum (bell pepper), chopped

¼ small red onion, sliced

½ small Lebanese or other small cucumber, halved lengthwise and sliced

20 g (¾ oz) mixed salad leaves

50 g (1¾ oz) fetta, crumbled

6 pitted kalamata olives

3 teaspoons olive oil

2 teaspoons red wine vinegar

For 2

300 g (10 oz) lamb leg steaks

1 clove garlic, crushed

1 teaspoon finely grated lemon zest

3 teaspoons lemon juice

½ teaspoon dried oregano

1 tablespoon olive oil

Greek-style salad

2 small tomatoes, cut into wedges

1 small red or green capsicum (bell pepper), chopped

½ small red onion, sliced

1 small Lebanese or other small cucumber, halved lengthwise and sliced

40 g (1½ oz) mixed salad leaves

100 g (3½ oz) fetta, crumbled

12 pitted kalamata olives

1 tablespoon olive oil

3 teaspoons red wine vinegar

Each serving provides
2540 kJ, 607 kcal, 45 g protein, 42 g fat (15 g saturated fat), 11 g carbohydrate (6 g sugars), 4 g fibre, 976 mg sodium

Cook's tips

Don't be put off by the long ingredient list — the salad is very adaptable, and you can add, replace or omit elements to suit.

Serve with crusty bread or warmed pita bread.

1 Cut the lamb across the grain into large cubes, about 2.5 cm (1 inch). Place in a shallow glass or ceramic dish, and toss with the garlic, lemon zest, lemon juice, oregano and olive oil. Cover and marinate at room temperature for 15 minutes.

2 To make the salad, combine the vegetables, salad leaves, fetta and olives in a bowl. Drizzle the oil and vinegar over and toss to coat.

3 Preheat a heavy-based frying pan over high heat. Cook lamb for 2–3 minutes on each side, or until it is brown and tender. Serve warm, with the salad.

Quick ideas for... one-pot pasta meals Couscous with

rian chilli beans LEMON AND SAFFRON RISOTTO step

deas for...one-pot pasta meals Pasta with fresh tomato a

Linguine with salmon and lemon cream

CK IDEAS FOR... ONE-POT PASTA MEALS Pasta prim

fron risotto step-by-step Macaroni bake Risoni ho

nean vegetable pilaf PASTA PRIMAVERA Oven-baked m

Creamy pumpkin penne Medite

grains, beans and pasta

Lemon and saffron risotto

Preparation 10 minutes

Cooking 30 minutes

For 1

3 teaspoons olive oil

½ small onion, finely chopped

1 small clove garlic, finely chopped

½ cup (110 g) risotto rice

1 cup (250 ml) hot chicken stock

a small pinch of saffron threads

juice and zest of ½ lemon

1½ tablespoons shaved parmesan

For 2

1 tablespoon olive oil

1 small onion, finely chopped

1 clove garlic, finely chopped

1 cup (220 g) risotto rice

2 cups (500 ml) hot chicken stock

a small pinch of saffron threads

juice and zest of 1 lemon

¼ cup (30 g) shaved parmesan

Each serving provides
2399 kJ, 573 kcal, 18 g protein, 15 g fat
(5 g saturated fat), 90 g carbohydrate
(4 g sugars), 1 g fibre, 859 mg sodium

Step 1 Heat the olive oil in a saucepan over medium heat. Add the onion, garlic and rice and cook for 3–4 minutes, stirring with a wooden spoon.

Step 2 Bring the stock to a gentle simmer with the saffron. Add a ladleful of stock to the rice, then stir for about 3 minutes, until the rice has absorbed almost all the liquid. Continue adding the stock, a ladleful at a time, until it is all absorbed and the rice is cooked to a creamy 'al dente' stage (about 20 minutes); you may need to add a little extra hot water.

Step 3 — Remove from the heat and stir in the lemon juice and lemon zest. Season to taste with salt and freshly ground black pepper. Place back over the heat for 1 minute, then stir the risotto again. Serve scattered with the parmesan and a good grind of pepper.

Grains, Beans and Pasta

Oven-baked mushroom and sausage pilaf

For 2

Preparation 5 minutes

Cooking 35 minutes

1 Preheat the oven to 180°C (350°F/Gas 4).

2 Meanwhile, heat the oil in a flameproof casserole dish over medium heat. Brown the sausages for 2 minutes, turning to ensure even browning. Remove from the dish, set aside and keep warm.

3 Cook the onion in the same dish for 3 minutes, or until softened. Add the mushrooms and cook for another 3 minutes, or until golden brown. Stir in the thyme and rice, then cook, stirring, for a further minute.

4 Return the sausages to the dish, pour in the stock and bring to a boil. Remove the dish from the heat and cover with a lid or a sheet of foil.

5 Transfer to the oven and bake for 25 minutes, or until the liquid has been absorbed and the rice is tender and cooked through. Serve hot.

2 teaspoons olive oil

6 beef chipolata sausages

1 small onion, chopped

200 g (7 oz) Swiss brown mushrooms, sliced

1 teaspoon fresh thyme leaves

½ cup (100 g) basmati rice

1 cup (250 ml) chicken stock

Each serving provides
2809 kJ, 671 kcal, 31 g protein, 42 g fat (18 g saturated fat), 53 g carbohydrate (3 g sugars), 3 g fibre, 1607 mg sodium

This dish is worth making for two as it keeps well. Simply refrigerate or freeze any leftovers and gently reheat for a quick meal another day.

Mediterranean vegetable pilaf

Quick

One-pot

For 2

Preparation 5 minutes + 3 minutes standing

Cooking 20 minutes

1 tablespoon olive oil

1 small onion, roughly chopped

1 teaspoon ground cumin

½ cup (100 g) basmati rice

1 cup (250 ml) chicken stock

280 g (10 oz) jar of chargrilled antipasto vegetables, drained well and chopped

1 tablespoon roughly chopped fresh parsley

lemon wedges, to serve

Each serving provides
1551 kJ, 370 kcal, 7 g protein, 17 g fat
(2 g saturated fat), 46 g carbohydrate
(3 g sugars), 2 g fibre, 646 mg sodium

1 Heat the oil in a frying pan over medium heat. Add the onion and cook for 2 minutes, or until softened. Add the cumin and rice and cook, stirring, for a further minute.

2 Pour in the stock and bring to a boil. Reduce the heat, cover with a lid and simmer for 15 minutes, or until the liquid has been absorbed and the rice is tender and cooked through. Turn off the heat.

3 Stir in the antipasto vegetables and parsley, then season with salt and freshly ground black pepper. Replace the lid and allow to stand for 3 minutes for the vegetables to heat through.

4 Serve in a bowl, with lemon wedges.

Cook's tip

Antipasto is sold in jars, and can also be purchased by weight from the delicatessen counter in supermarkets.

Another idea

Instead of antipasto, use fresh chopped vegetables of your choice. Sauté them with the onion in step 1.

Couscous with prawns and zucchini

Preparation 10 minutes

Cooking 10 minutes

For 1

5 raw prawns (uncooked shrimp), about 150 g (5 oz)

½ cup (100 g) instant couscous

½ cup (125 ml) boiling chicken stock

2 teaspoons olive oil

½ small red onion, sliced

½ zucchini (courgette), sliced diagonally

1 small clove garlic, crushed

30 g (1 oz) marinated fetta

fresh mint leaves, to serve

For 2

10 raw prawns (uncooked shrimp), about 300 g (10 oz)

1 cup (200 g) instant couscous

1 cup (250 ml) boiling chicken stock

1 tablespoon olive oil

1 small red onion, sliced

1 zucchini (courgette), sliced diagonally

1 clove garlic, crushed

60 g (2 oz) marinated fetta

fresh mint leaves, to serve

1 Peel and devein the prawns, leaving the tail intact. Discard the head and shells and set the prawn meat aside.

2 Place the couscous in a small bowl, pour the hot stock over and cover with plastic wrap.

3 Meanwhile, heat half the oil in a small frying pan over medium heat. Sauté the onion and zucchini for 3 minutes, or until softened and lightly golden. Add the garlic and cook for a further minute. Remove the mixture from the pan, set aside and keep warm.

4 Heat the remaining oil in the same frying pan. Add the prawns and cook for 1–2 minutes on each side, or until they turn bright orange and are cooked through. Stir the onion and zucchini

mixture through. Season to taste with salt and freshly ground black pepper.

5 Fluff the couscous grains using a fork, add the prawns and vegetables, then crumble the fetta over. Drizzle with the fetta marinating oil, scatter with mint, lightly toss and serve.

Leftover magic

Leftover uncooked couscous can be stored in an airtight container in the pantry for several months.

Each serving provides
1931 kJ, 461 kcal, 42 g protein, 21 g fat (8 g saturated fat), 26 g carbohydrate (3 g sugars), 1 g fibre, 913 mg sodium

Vegetarian chilli beans

Quick

One-pot

For 2

Preparation 10 minutes

- -

Cooking 15 minutes

2 teaspoons olive oil

1 small onion, chopped

1 clove garlic, crushed

½ teaspoon paprika

½ teaspoon ground cumin

½ teaspoon dried red chilli flakes

410 g (15 oz) can chopped tomatoes

⅔ cup (100 g) chopped roasted capsicum (bell pepper)

420 g (15 oz) can red kidney beans, rinsed and drained

half a 300 g (10 oz) jar tomato salsa

2 spring onions (scallions), diagonally sliced

1 tablespoon chopped fresh parsley

crusty bread or steamed rice, to serve (optional)

- -

Each serving provides
1069 kJ, 255 kcal, 12 g protein, 8 g fat
(1 g saturated fat), 33 g carbohydrate
(16 g sugars), 13 g fibre, 892 mg sodium

1 Heat the oil in a saucepan over medium heat. Add the onion and cook for 3 minutes, or until softened. Stir in the garlic, spices and chilli flakes and cook for a further minute.

2 Stir in the tomato, capsicum, beans and salsa and bring to a boil. Reduce the heat and simmer for 10 minutes, or until the mixture has thickened, stirring occasionally.

3 Sprinkle with the spring onions and parsley and serve with crusty bread or steamed rice, if desired.

Roasted capsicum can be bought in jars and at the delicatessen counter in supermarkets. Drain off the oil before using.

Other ideas

- Cook 250 g (8 oz) lean minced (ground) beef with the onion, then continue with the recipe.
- Top the chilli beans with diced avocado, a dollop of sour cream or some fresh chopped coriander (cilantro) instead of parsley.
- Use the chilli beans as a filling for a warmed tortilla, with some shredded lettuce, sour cream and avocado.

Leftover magic

- If cooking for one, freeze the leftover chilli in an airtight container. Thaw it in the fridge for 24 hours before reheating.
- Tomato salsa keeps well in the fridge for a week or two. Serve it as a simple dip with corn chips, perhaps with some fresh chopped coriander (cilantro) mixed through.

Quick ideas for... one-pot pasta meals

Pop a pan of water on the stove, bring it to a boil and throw in some pasta. Grab a few simple ingredients and hey presto, dinner is served! These recipes serve 1; double the ingredients to serve 2.

Cooking perfect pasta

Different shapes and sizes of pasta have different cooking times. Check your packet for instructions, though it is best to taste-test a piece just before the recommended cooking time is up, to ensure you don't overcook it. Pasta should be 'al dente', which literally means 'to the tooth' — tender but not mushy. Feel free to use different pasta shapes to those given in the recipes.

As a rule of thumb, use 100 g (3½ oz) dried pasta per person, though appetites vary. Even when cooking for only one, use a large pot. Bring the water to a boil, stir in a good pinch of salt, then add the pasta. Cook until al dente, drain, and use as directed.

Fresh tomato sauce

Cook **rigatoni** as directed; drain and return to the pot. Chop 2 small ripe **tomatoes** and mix with 2 teaspoons **balsamic vinegar**, 1 tablespoon extra virgin **olive oil**, 1 small crushed **garlic** clove (optional) and 1 tablespoon shredded **fresh basil**. Toss through the warm pasta, season well with salt and freshly ground black pepper and serve.

Chicken and pesto

Cook **farfalle** as directed; drain and return to the pot. Immediately add 1 tablespoon **basil pesto** and toss to coat. Mix in ½ cup (90 g) shredded cooked or barbecued **chicken** and ½ cup (65 g) halved **cherry tomatoes**. Season with salt and freshly ground black pepper and serve.

Chilli tuna penne

Cook **penne** as directed; drain and set aside. Pour the **oil** from a 95 g (3 oz) can of **tuna** into the pasta cooking pot. Add 1 small crushed **garlic** clove and ¼ teaspoon chopped **chilli** (from a jar). Sauté over medium heat for about 30 seconds, then turn off the heat. Return the pasta to the pan. Use a fork to flake the tuna, then add to the pasta, along with ½ cup (10 g) torn **rocket (arugula) leaves**, 1 teaspoon **baby capers** and 1 tablespoon **lemon juice**, to taste. Season with salt and freshly ground black pepper and serve.

Cook's tip If you have tuna in chilli oil, leave out the chopped chilli.

Spinach and fetta

Cook **fusilli** as directed; drain and return to the pot. Toss with 1 tablespoon extra virgin **olive oil** and ⅔ cup (30 g) shredded **baby English spinach leaves** until the leaves wilt. Add ¼ cup (40 g) chopped **roasted red capsicum (bell pepper)**, 40 g (1½ oz) crumbled **fetta** and 3 teaspoons toasted **pine nuts**. Gently toss together and serve.

Tortellini margarita

Cook **tortellini** as directed; drain and set aside. Heat 1 tablespoon **olive oil** in the pasta cooking pot. Add 1 small crushed **garlic** clove and 6 halved **cherry tomatoes**. Sauté over medium heat for 3 minutes, or until the tomatoes have softened. Turn off the heat and return the pasta to the pot. Fold the pasta through, along with 2 tablespoons shredded **basil** and ¼ cup (35 g) grated **mozzarella**. Season with salt and freshly ground black pepper and serve.

Pasta is generally low in fat and rich in complex carbohydrates. Inexpensive and easy to cook, it is an invaluable pantry item.

Ham and zucchini spaghetti

Cook **spaghetti** as directed, adding ¼ cup (40 g) thawed frozen **peas** for the last 2 minutes of cooking. Drain and set aside. Heat 1 tablespoon **olive oil** in the pasta cooking pot. Add 1 sliced **spring onion** (scallion) and 1 small grated **zucchini** (courgette) and sauté for 2 minutes, or until tender. Return the pasta and peas to the pot. Add 2 tablespoons **reduced-fat cream cheese** and 50 g (1¾ oz) chopped **ham** and toss over medium heat for 2–3 minutes, or until evenly combined. Season with salt and freshly ground black pepper and serve.

Cook's tip Thaw the peas by immersing them in hot water before adding them to the pot, so the cooking temperature doesn't drop too much.

Antipasto delight

Cook **tagliatelle** as directed; drain and return to the pot. Add 3 chopped **artichoke hearts**, 2 tablespoons chopped pitted **kalamata olives**, ¼ cup (30 g) chopped **semi-dried (sun-blushed) tomatoes**, 50 g (1¾ oz) chopped **salami** and 2 tablespoons chopped **fresh parsley**. Season with salt and freshly ground black pepper and toss well. Serve sprinkled with grated **parmesan**.

Linguine with salmon and lemon cream

Preparation 10 minutes

Cooking 15 minutes

For 1

100 g (3½ oz) linguine

1 teaspoon olive oil

2 spring onions (scallions), sliced

1 small clove garlic, crushed

⅓ cup (80 ml) cream

¼ teaspoon dijon mustard

¼ teaspoon finely grated lemon zest

½ teaspoon lemon juice

60 g (2 oz) portion hot smoked salmon, flaked into big chunks

snipped fresh chives, to garnish

For 2

200 g (7 oz) linguine

2 teaspoons olive oil

4 spring onions (scallions), sliced

1 clove garlic, crushed

⅔ cup (160 ml) cream

½ teaspoon dijon mustard

½ teaspoon finely grated lemon zest

1 teaspoon lemon juice

125 g (4 oz) portion hot smoked salmon, flaked into big chunks

snipped fresh chives, to garnish

1 Cook the pasta in a saucepan of salted boiling water following the packet instructions.

2 Meanwhile, heat the oil in a frying pan over medium heat. Add the spring onions and garlic and cook for 1 minute. Pour in the cream, then stir the mustard and lemon zest through. Bring to a boil, add the lemon juice and salmon, then reduce the heat and simmer for 1 minute.

3 Drain the pasta, return to the pan and stir the salmon and lemon cream sauce mixture through. Serve sprinkled with chives.

Other ideas

▧ Replace the salmon with smoked trout or cold smoked salmon slices.

▧ Instead of linguine, use angel hair pasta or spaghetti.

Leftover magic

▧ Use any leftover salmon or trout in the **Scrambled eggs with salmon** on page 44.

Each serving provides
3249 kJ, 776 kcal, 28 g protein, 42 g fat (23 g saturated fat), 72 g carbohydrate (4 g sugars), 4 g fibre, 1132 mg sodium

Pasta with fresh tomato and walnuts

Preparation 5 minutes

Cooking 15 minutes

For 1

100 g (3½ oz) pappardelle pasta

2 teaspoons olive oil

125 g (4 oz) cherry tomatoes, halved

1 small clove garlic, crushed

2 tablespoons toasted walnuts

a squeeze of lemon juice

2 teaspoons finely grated parmesan

5 small basil leaves

For 2

200 g (7 oz) pappardelle pasta

1 tablespoon olive oil

250 g (8 oz) cherry tomatoes, halved

1 clove garlic, crushed

⅓ cup (40 g) toasted walnuts

a good squeeze of lemon juice

1 tablespoon finely grated parmesan

10 small basil leaves

1 Cook the pasta in a saucepan of salted boiling water according to the packet instructions.

2 Meanwhile, heat the oil in a frying pan over high heat. Add the tomatoes and cook, stirring occasionally, for 2 minutes, or until softened and lightly seared on the edges. Stir in the garlic and walnuts until heated through.

3 Drain the pasta and return to the pan, then stir in the tomato mixture.

4 Serve in bowls with a squeeze of lemon juice, sprinkled with the parmesan and basil.

Other ideas

▬ This dish can also be eaten as a salad. Cook the pasta and allow it to cool. Do not cook the tomatoes or heat the toasted walnuts. Instead, toss them together in a bowl with the remaining ingredients, then stir the mixture through the cooled pasta.

▬ Olives can be added to this recipe.

Each serving provides
2443 kJ, 584 kcal, 16 g protein, 25 g fat (3 g saturated fat), 72 g carbohydrate (4 g sugars), 7 g fibre, 68 mg sodium

Other ideas

- For a vegetarian version, omit the bacon.
- Replace the bacon with prosciutto, salami or pancetta — fry until crisp and drain on paper towel.
- Reduced-fat cream can be used in this recipe.

Creamy pumpkin penne

Preparation 10 minutes

Cooking 15 minutes

For 1

- 100 g (3½ oz) penne pasta
- 100 g (3½ oz) butternut pumpkin (winter squash), peeled and cut into small cubes
- 2 teaspoons olive oil
- ½ small onion, chopped
- 1 small clove garlic, crushed
- ⅓ cup (80 ml) cream
- 1 tablespoon sliced sun-dried tomatoes
- 2 teaspoons toasted pine nuts
- ½ teaspoon chopped fresh sage
- 1 slice rindless bacon (bacon strip), fried and chopped

For 2

- 200 g (7 oz) penne pasta
- 200 g (7 oz) butternut pumpkin (winter squash), peeled and cut into small cubes
- 1 tablespoon olive oil
- 1 small onion, chopped
- 1 clove garlic, crushed
- ⅔ cup (160 ml) cream
- 2 tablespoons sliced sun-dried tomatoes
- 1 tablespoon toasted pine nuts
- 1 teaspoon chopped fresh sage
- 2 slices rindless bacon (bacon strips), fried and chopped

1 Cook the pasta in a saucepan of salted boiling water according to the packet instructions, adding the pumpkin during the last 5 minutes.

2 Meanwhile, heat the oil in a frying pan over medium heat. Add the onion and garlic and cook for 2 minutes. Pour in the cream, then stir in the tomatoes, pine nuts and sage. Bring to a boil, reduce the heat and simmer for 1 minute.

3 Drain the pasta and pumpkin and return to the pan. Gently stir the sauce through. Serve topped with the bacon.

Leftover magic

- Leftover pine nuts can be refrigerated in an airtight container and used in other recipes, or for making pesto.
- You can use leftover roasted pumpkin and other vegetables – chop them, then warm them through in the creamy sauce.

Each serving provides
3805 kJ, 909 kcal, 25 g protein, 53 g fat (25 g saturated fat), 86 g carbohydrate (8 g sugars), 7 g fibre, 678 mg sodium

Risoni hotpot

Preparation 10 minutes

Cooking 15 minutes

For 1

1 teaspoon olive oil

½ small onion, sliced

1 small clove garlic, crushed

45 g (1½ oz) sliced salami, roughly chopped

half a 410 g (15 oz) can chopped tomatoes

1 cup (250 ml) chicken stock

¼ cup (40 g) risoni pasta

60 g (2 oz) marinated artichoke quarters

1 tablespoon sliced black olives

2 teaspoons chopped fresh parsley

For 2

2 teaspoons olive oil

1 small onion, sliced

1 clove garlic, crushed

90 g (3 oz) sliced salami, roughly chopped

410 g (15 oz) can chopped tomatoes

2 cups (500 ml) chicken stock

½ cup (80 g) risoni pasta

125 g (4 oz) marinated artichoke quarters

2 tablespoons sliced black olives

1 tablespoon chopped fresh parsley

1 Heat the oil in a small saucepan. Add the onion and cook over medium heat for 3 minutes, or until softened. Add the garlic and salami and cook for a further 1 minute.

2 Pour in the tomatoes and stock and bring to a boil. Add the risoni and simmer for 8 minutes, stirring occasionally to stop the pasta sticking to the base of the pan.

3 Stir the artichoke and olives through and simmer for 2 minutes. Sprinkle with the parsley and serve.

Leftover magic

Leftover uncooked risoni will keep in an airtight container in the pantry for several months.

Cook's tips

You can buy marinated artichokes by weight from the delicatessen section of supermarkets. For a heartier meal, also add some chopped roasted red capsicum (bell pepper), eggplant (aubergine) and sun-dried tomatoes.

Each serving provides
2245 kJ, 536 kcal, 21 g protein, 30 g fat (7 g saturated fat), 43 g carbohydrate (11 g sugars), 6 g fibre, 1840 mg sodium

Other ideas

- Use any small pasta shapes in this recipe.
- Use any combination of spring vegetables, such as broad (fava) beans, squash and baby green beans.

Pasta primavera

Preparation 10 minutes

Cooking 20 minutes

For 1

75 g (2½ oz) farfalle pasta

3 asparagus spears, cut into 3 cm (1¼ inch) lengths

¼ cup (40 g) frozen peas, thawed

½ small zucchini (courgette), sliced

4 snow peas (mangetout), sliced in half diagonally

⅓ cup (80 ml) cream

1 small clove garlic, crushed

½ teaspoon finely grated lemon zest

shaved parmesan, to serve

fresh mint leaves, to garnish

For 2

150 g (5 oz) farfalle pasta

6 asparagus spears, cut into 3 cm (1¼ inch) lengths

⅓ cup (55 g) frozen peas, thawed

1 small zucchini (courgette), sliced

8 snow peas (mangetout), sliced in half diagonally

⅔ cup (160 ml) cream

1 clove garlic, crushed

1 teaspoon finely grated lemon zest

shaved parmesan, to serve

fresh mint leaves, to garnish

1 Cook the pasta in a saucepan of salted boiling water following the packet instructions.

2 Meanwhile, bring another saucepan of water to a boil. Add the asparagus, peas and zucchini and cook for 1 minute. Add the snow peas and cook for another minute. Drain and refresh the vegetables under cold running water so they keep their vibrant colour. Drain well.

3 Place the pan back over medium heat. Pour in the cream, then stir in the garlic and lemon zest and bring to a boil. Add the blanched vegetables and simmer for 2 minutes. Season with salt and freshly ground black pepper.

4 Drain the pasta and return to the pan. Gently stir the sauce through. Serve topped with parmesan and garnished with mint.

Leftover magic

- Any leftover asparagus can be added to the **Lemon and saffron risotto** on page 180.
- Leftover cream can be used in the **Mini bread and butter pudding** on page 236.

Each serving provides
2437 kJ, 582 kcal, 13 g protein, 34 g fat (22 g saturated fat), 56 g carbohydrate (4 g sugars), 4 g fibre, 31 mg sodium

Macaroni bake

Preparation 10 minutes
- -
Cooking 25 minutes

For 1

½ cup (80 g) macaroni

¼ cup (40 g) frozen peas

1 tablespoon butter

2 teaspoons plain (all-purpose)
    flour

¾ cup (180 ml) milk

¼ teaspoon finely grated lemon
    zest

a pinch of nutmeg

¼ cup (30 g) grated cheddar

1 tablespoon finely grated
    parmesan

¼ cup (20 g) fresh breadcrumbs

20 g (¾ oz) goat's cheese

For 2

1 cup (150 g) macaroni

½ cup (80 g) frozen peas

2 tablespoons butter

1 tablespoon plain (all-purpose)
    flour

1½ cups (375 ml) milk

½ teaspoon finely grated lemon
    zest

a pinch of nutmeg

½ cup (60 g) grated cheddar

2 tablespoons finely grated
    parmesan

½ cup (40 g) fresh breadcrumbs

40 g (1½ oz) goat's cheese

1 Preheat the oven to 180°C (350°F/Gas 4).

2 Cook the pasta in a saucepan of salted boiling water according to the packet instructions, adding the peas during the last 4 minutes.

3 Meanwhile, melt the butter in a small saucepan over low heat. Add the flour and stir for 1 minute. Remove from the heat and gradually pour in the milk, stirring until smooth.

4 Return the pan to the heat. Add the lemon zest and nutmeg and stir until the sauce boils and thickens. Stir in the cheddar and parmesan, reduce the heat and simmer for 3 minutes. Season with salt and freshly ground black pepper.

5 Drain the pasta and peas, then return them to the pan. Stir the cheese sauce through.

6 Spoon the mixture into one or two small (1 cup) ovenproof dishes. Sprinkle with the breadcrumbs and crumble the goat's cheese over. Bake for 10–12 minutes, or until the breadcrumbs are golden brown.

- -

Each serving provides
3879 kJ, 927 kcal, 38 g protein, 44 g fat (28 g saturated fat), 95 g carbohydrate (12 g sugars), 4 g fibre, 899 mg sodium

Cook's tips

Mix some chopped salami or cooked bacon through the macaroni.

Buy grated cheese from the supermarket and freeze it in zip-lock bags. It's easy to then remove the amount needed for each recipe.

Cherry and almond sundae   Ricotta pancakes with

uick ideas for... stewed fruit POACHED PEARS STEP-BY-STE But

lk pancakes   Step-by-step   Quick and healthy muffins

ted strawberries   French toast   Banana and strawberr

UICK IDEAS FOR... STEWED FRUIT   Spiced fruit and

Rice pudding   Poached pears Step-by-step   Macerated straw

Quick ideas for... stewed fruit   Trifle Berry whip

Refrigerator biscuits   RICE PUDDING   Banana bread Baked b

sweet treats

Refrigerator biscuits

Makes 50

Preparation 20 minutes + 1 hour resting

Cooking 10 minutes

250 g (8 oz) butter, at room
temperature

1 cup (125 g) icing
(confectioners') sugar, sifted

2½ cups (375 g) plain
(all-purpose) flour

½ cup (90 g) dried apricots,
finely chopped

½ cup (70 g) roasted hazelnuts
(filberts), finely chopped

Each biscuit provides
353 kJ, 84 kcal, 1 g protein, 5 g fat
(3 g saturated fat), 8 g carbohydrate
(3 g sugars), <1 g fibre, 36 mg sodium

1 Using electric beaters, beat the butter and icing sugar in a bowl until light and creamy. Transfer to a large bowl.

2 Sift the flour over the butter mixture, then stir it in, using a large metal spoon, until well combined. Gently mix the apricots and hazelnuts through.

3 Turn the dough out onto a lightly floured surface and knead until smooth. Divide the dough in half, then roll each piece into a log about 25 cm (10 inches) long. Wrap each log in baking (parchment) paper or plastic wrap and refrigerate for 1 hour, or until firm. (Alternatively, refrigerate the logs for up to 10 days, or freeze for up to 3 months.)

4 Preheat the oven to 180°C (350°F/Gas 4). Line two baking trays with baking paper.

5 Cut each log into slices 1 cm (½ inch) thick, placing them on the baking trays about 3 cm (1¼ inches) apart. Bake for 10 minutes, or until firm and cooked through.

6 Remove from the oven and leave to cool on the trays. Store in airtight containers.

Cook's tip

The beauty of this recipe is that the unbaked dough will keep in the fridge for 7–10 days, or can be frozen for up to 3 months. The idea is that you can bake up a fresh batch any time you like, without having to make new dough each time. The biscuits (cookies) only take about 10 minutes to bake.

Other ideas

Replace the apricots and hazelnuts with other fruit and nuts – try craisins and pistachio nuts.

Banana bread

Makes 1 loaf

Preparation 15 minutes
- -
Cooking 50 minutes

1 Preheat the oven to 180°C (350°F/Gas 4). Lightly grease a 21 x 10 cm (8¼ x 4 inch) loaf (bar) tin, then line it with baking (parchment) paper.

2 Combine the flours, sugar, coconut and cinnamon in a large bowl. Make a well in the centre.

3 Whisk together the eggs, banana, buttermilk and oil. Add to the flour mixture and stir until just combined. Spoon the mixture into the loaf tin.

4 Bake for 45–50 minutes, or until a skewer inserted in the centre of the loaf comes out clean. Remove from the oven and leave in the tin for 5 minutes, before turning out onto a wire rack to cool completely.

Another idea

Add chocolate chips or frozen raspberries or blueberries to the mixture before spooning it into the tin.

1½ cups (225 g) self-raising flour

⅓ cup (50 g) plain (all-purpose) flour

¾ cup (140 g) brown sugar

⅓ cup (30 g) desiccated coconut

1 teaspoon ground cinnamon

2 eggs, lightly whisked

3 ripe bananas, mashed; about 1 cup (240 g)

½ cup (125 ml) buttermilk

⅓ cup (80 ml) canola oil

- -

Each slice provides
888 kJ, 212 kcal, 4 g protein, 9 g fat
(2 g saturated fat), 29 g carbohydrate
(15 g sugars), 2 g fibre, 128 mg sodium

The banana bread will remain fresh for 3–4 days if stored in an airtight container. It also freezes well: wrap individual slices in plastic wrap for easy retrieval, then thaw or toast as desired.

Spiced fruit and nut bread

Makes 1 loaf

Preparation 10 minutes

Cooking 40 minutes

1½ cups (225 g) self-raising flour

¼ cup (55 g) caster (superfine)
 sugar

1 teaspoon ground cinnamon

½ teaspoon mixed (pumpkin pie)
 spice

1 cup (185 g) dried fruit medley

¼ cup (25 g) flaked almonds

1 egg

70 g (2½ oz) butter, melted

½ cup (125 ml) milk

Each slice provides
707 kJ, 169 kcal, 3 g protein, 7 g fat
(4 g saturated fat), 23 g carbohydrate
(12 g sugars), 1 g fibre, 167 mg sodium

1 Preheat the oven to 180°C (350°F/Gas 4). Lightly grease a 21 x 10 cm (8¼ x 4 inch) loaf (bar) tin, then line it with baking (parchment) paper.

2 Combine the flour, sugar, cinnamon, mixed spice, dried fruit and almonds in a bowl. Make a well in the centre.

3 Whisk together the egg, butter and milk. Add to the flour mixture and stir until just combined, then spoon the mixture into the loaf tin.

4 Bake for 35–40 minutes, or until a skewer inserted in the centre of the loaf comes out clean. Remove from the oven and leave in the tin for 5 minutes, before turning out onto a wire rack to cool completely.

Cook's tips

■ Dried fruit medley is a mixture of sultanas (golden raisins), dried apricots, apples, peaches and pears, and is available from most supermarkets. Alternatively, make up your own mixture of dried fruits.

■ It's best to use a serrated knife when cutting this loaf.

Leftover magic

This lovely bread will remain fresh for 3–4 days if stored in an airtight container. It also freezes well: wrap individual slices in plastic wrap for easy retrieval, then thaw or toast as desired.

Quick and healthy muffins

Makes 6	Preparation 10 minutes
	Cooking 20 minutes

1 Preheat the oven to 200°C (400°F/Gas 6). Line a 6-hole standard muffin tin with paper cases.

2 Sift the flours into a bowl, adding the husks to the bowl.

3 In another bowl, whisk together the eggs, oil, honey and milk. Add to the flour mixture and stir until just combined. Gently fold the raspberries through.

4 Spoon the mixture evenly into the muffin cases, until they are two-thirds full. Bake for 18–20 minutes, or until the muffins are cooked and golden.

5 Remove from the oven and leave in the tin for 5 minutes, before turning out onto a wire rack to cool completely.

Cook's tip

Use frozen berries if fresh berries are unavailable.

Other ideas

Replace the raspberries with blueberries, dried fruit, sultanas (golden raisins), cranberries or choc chips.

1 cup (150 g) self-raising flour
½ cup (75 g) wholemeal (whole-wheat) self-raising flour
2 eggs, lightly whisked
½ cup (125 ml) light olive oil
½ cup (175 g) honey
⅓ cup (80 ml) milk
1 cup (125 g) fresh raspberries

Each muffin provides
1723 kJ, 412 kcal, 3 g protein, 22 g fat
(4 g saturated fat), 49 g carbohydrate
(26 g sugars), 3 g fibre, 260 mg sodium

These scrumptious muffins will keep in an airtight container for several days, or can be frozen in zip-lock bags for later enjoyment.

Buttermilk pancakes

Preparation 10 minutes +
5 minutes standing

Cooking 10 minutes

For 2

½ cup (75 g) self-raising flour

2 teaspoons sugar

¼ teaspoon bicarbonate of soda
   (baking soda)

¾ cup (180 ml) low-fat buttermilk

1 tablespoon vegetable oil

1 small egg

½ teaspoon vanilla extract

1½ tablespoons maple syrup

fresh berries in season, such as
   raspberries, to serve

Each serving (4 pancakes) provides
1652 kJ, 394 kcal, 11 g protein, 13 g fat
(3 g saturated fat), 58 g carbohydrate
(30 g sugars), 3 g fibre, 669 mg sodium

The batter works best when made for two people, but you can easily freeze any leftover pancakes for another day.

Step 1   Whisk the flour, sugar and bicarbonate of soda in a bowl; make a well in the centre. Whisk the buttermilk, oil, egg and vanilla into the flour mixture until just incorporated. Allow to stand for 5 minutes.

Step 2   Coat a non-stick frying pan with cooking oil spray and set over medium heat until hot but not smoking. For each pancake, pour in about 2 tablespoons of batter.

Step 3 Cook for 3 minutes, or until the bubbles around the pancake edges start to burst. Flip the pancakes over and cook for another 1–2 minutes, or until golden underneath. Serve warm, topped with raspberries and syrup.

Ricotta pancakes with fresh fruit

Preparation 10 minutes

Cooking 5–10 minutes

For 1

1 egg

2 teaspoons caster (superfine) sugar

2 tablespoons ricotta (about 40 g)

1 tablespoon milk

¼ cup (35 g) self-raising flour

butter, for pan-frying

¼ banana, sliced

2 strawberries, sliced

2 teaspoons roughly chopped walnuts

1 tablespoon natural (plain) yogurt

2 teaspoons warmed honey

For 2

2 eggs

1 tablespoon caster (superfine) sugar

4 tablespoons ricotta (about 80 g)

2 tablespoons milk

½ cup (75 g) self-raising flour

butter, for pan-frying

½ banana, sliced

4 strawberries, sliced

1 tablespoon roughly chopped walnuts

2 tablespoons natural (plain) yogurt

1 tablespoon warmed honey

1 In a bowl, whisk together the egg, sugar, ricotta and milk until well combined. Add the flour and stir until well combined.

2 Melt some butter in a large non-stick frying pan over medium heat. Making three pancakes for each person, spoon the mixture into the pan. Using the back of a spoon, spread the mixture out to make circles of about 10 cm (4 inches). (If cooking for two, you will need to cook the pancakes in two batches.)

3 Cook the pancakes for 2 minutes, or until small bubbles appear on the surface. Turn and cook the other side for a further 1–2 minutes, or until cooked and golden.

4 Serve the pancakes warm, with the banana, strawberries and walnuts, topped with the yogurt and drizzled with the honey.

Cook's tip

To warm honey for drizzling, heat it in the microwave for a few seconds.

Each serving provides
1745 kJ, 417 kcal, 17 g protein, 17 g fat (7 g saturated fat), 50 g carbohydrate (28 g sugars), 3 g fibre, 399 mg sodium

French toast

Preparation 10 minutes

Cooking 5–10 minutes

For 1

3 slices white bread

1 egg

2 tablespoons milk

2 teaspoons butter

2 teaspoons caster (superfine)
  sugar

¼ teaspoon ground cinnamon

4 strawberries, sliced

2 teaspoons maple syrup

For 2

6 slices white bread

2 eggs

4 tablespoons milk

1 tablespoon butter

1 tablespoon caster (superfine)
  sugar

½ teaspoon ground cinnamon

8 strawberries, sliced

1 tablespoon maple syrup

1 Using an 8.5 cm (3½ inch) round cutter, cut out a round from each slice of bread. Whisk together the egg and milk in a shallow, wide dish. Dip the bread into the egg mixture, turning to coat.

2 Melt the butter in a large non-stick frying pan over medium heat. Remove the bread from the egg mixture, allowing any excess to drip off. Working in two batches if necessary, fry the bread slices for 1–2 minutes on each side, or until golden brown. Sprinkle with the combined sugar and cinnamon.

3 Arrange a round of French toast on each serving plate and top with a few strawberry slices. Repeat with the remaining French toast rounds and strawberries. Drizzle with the maple syrup and serve immediately.

Cook's tip

Experiment with different shaped cutters, such as star-shaped cutters.

Other ideas

- Use sliced banana and mixed berries instead of the strawberries.
- Turn this into a dessert and serve with a scoop of ice-cream.

Each serving provides
2268 kJ, 542 kcal, 19 g protein, 18 g fat (8 g saturated fat), 76 g carbohydrate (23 g sugars), 5 g fibre, 771 mg sodium

Quick ideas for... stewed fruit

Stewing is a simple way to preserve fruit. The two base recipes below serve 8 and are lovely with cream, ice cream or custard. The recipes opposite use up 2 serves of each base recipe; halve them to serve 1.

Stewed apples or pears

8 granny smith apples or pears
1/3 cup (80 g) caster (superfine) sugar

1 Peel and quarter the fruit. Cut out the cores, then cut each piece in half again. Place in a medium–large saucepan with the sugar, cinnamon stick and 2 tablespoons water.

2 Cover and cook over medium heat for 5 minutes, stirring occasionally, until soft. Remove the cinnamon stick.

Freezing stewed fruit

Cool completely, divide in portions for 1 or 2, place in zip-lock bags and expel the air. Label, date and freeze for 6 months. Thaw in a microwave, or overnight in fridge.

Stewed rhubarb and strawberries

12 rhubarb stalks (about 500 g/1 lb)
400 g (14 oz) strawberries
1/4 cup (55 g) caster (superfine) sugar
1 vanilla bean, cut in half lengthwise

1 Discard the ends and leaves from the rhubarb, then chop the stalks into 2 cm (3/4 inch) lengths. Place in a medium–large saucepan with the remaining ingredients and 1/4 cup (60 ml) water. Stir over medium–low heat until the sugar has dissolved.

2 Cover and gently simmer for 5–6 minutes, or until the rhubarb is tender but not falling apart. Remove the vanilla bean.

Cook's tip Vanilla beans are expensive, but can be reused. Rinse, pat dry with paper towels, then allow to air dry and store in an airtight container. Alternatively, use 1 teaspoon vanilla extract.

Other fruits

Soft fruits such as peaches, nectarines, plums and apricots are also great stewed and frozen. The cooking time will depend on the ripeness of the fruit.

For 1.5 kg (3 lb) fruit, combine 4 cups (1 litre) water and 1 cup (220 g) sugar in a large saucepan over low heat. Stir until the sugar dissolves, bring to a simmer, then add the fruit. Return to a simmer and cook for 5 minutes, or until soft. Lift the fruit out with a slotted spoon and cool slightly. Slip off the skins if you like (they will remove easily from peaches, but others can be left on), and cut the fruit from the stones. Makes 8 serves.

Fruit crumble

Preheat the oven to 200°C (400°F/Gas 6). Spoon 2 serves of **stewed fruit** into a 2 cup (500 ml) ovenproof dish, or two 1 cup (250 ml) dishes. In a bowl, combine 2 tablespoons **untoasted muesli** or **rolled (porridge) oats**, 1½ tablespoons **plain (all-purpose) flour**, 2 teaspoons **brown sugar** and 1 tablespoon **butter**. Rub in the butter with your fingertips until well combined, then sprinkle over the fruit. Bake for 12–15 minutes, or until golden.

Turnovers

Preheat the oven to 200°C (400°F/Gas 6) and line a baking tray with baking paper. Cut a thawed sheet of frozen **puff pastry** into four squares. Place half a **stewed fruit** portion on each piece, then fold over diagonally to form a triangle. Press and seal the edges together with a fork. Place on the baking tray, brush with lightly beaten **egg white** and sprinkle lightly with **caster (superfine) sugar**. Bake for 15 minutes, or until golden brown. The turnovers will keep for 1 day in an airtight container, and can be reheated.

Trifle

Layer two 1¼ cup (310 ml) glasses with 1 cup (250 ml) ready-made **custard**, 1 cup (100 g) chopped **plain cake** (or 2 sliced jam rollettes/ mini jelly rolls) and **stewed fruit**, alternating the layers and sprinkling the cake layers with a little **sherry** if you like. Refrigerate for at least 1 hour, for the flavours to merge. Serve as is, or top with a spoonful of **thick (heavy/double) cream** or **whipped cream** and toasted **slivered almonds**.

Cherry and apple strudel

Preheat the oven to 200°C (400°F/Gas 6) and line a baking tray with baking paper. Combine **stewed apples** with 100 g (3½ oz) pitted **fresh cherries**. Melt 2 tablespoons **butter** and lightly brush over a sheet of **filo pastry**. Lay another sheet of filo on top, then brush with more butter. Repeat twice more, to make four layers. Arrange the cherry mixture along one short end of pastry, about 4 cm (1½ inches) in from the edge. Fold the end of the filo over the fruit, then fold the sides in. Roll up to enclose the filling, then place on the baking tray, seam side down. Brush with the remaining butter and sprinkle with 1 tablespoon **flaked almonds**. Bake for 12–15 minutes, until golden brown. Dust with **icing (confectioners') sugar** before serving.

More ideas for stewed fruit

- Serve for breakfast with muesli (page 13), porridge (page 13) or other cereal.
- Serve with Rice pudding (page 227), over pancakes (see pages 214 and 217) or with French toast (page 218).
- Fill ready-made meringue nests with whipped cream and top with stewed fruit.
- Mix fresh ricotta with a little sugar and vanilla extract. Spread over warm crepes, top with stewed fruit and roll up to enclose.

Berry whip

Preparation 4 minutes

Cooking None

Quick

No-Cook

For 1

150 g (5 oz) frozen berries

150 g (5 oz) frozen yogurt

1 teaspoon icing
(confectioners') sugar

For 2

300 g (10 oz) frozen berries

300 g (10 oz) frozen yogurt

2 teaspoons icing
(confectioners') sugar

Each serving provides
1470 kJ, 351 kcal, 9 g protein, 10 g fat (7 g saturated fat),
55 g carbohydrate (49 g sugars), 6 g fibre, 94 mg sodium

1 Place the frozen berries, yogurt and icing sugar in a blender and mix until smooth.

2 Serve immediately, in a tall glass or glasses.

Cook's tip

Any fresh seasonal berries can be used instead of frozen berries.

Other ideas

- Use frozen cherries or mango instead of berries, and experiment with different flavours of frozen yogurt.
- Make an 'Eton mess' by serving the berry whip in a bowl with crushed ready-made meringues.
- Here's another no-cook dessert idea. For two people, pour 1 cup (250 ml) ready-made low-fat custard into a bowl. In a blender, purée 200 g (7 oz) canned fruit — try cherries, apricots, peaches, plums, mango or even fruit salad mixes. Stir the puréed fruit into the custard. Divide among two small glasses and chill in the freezer for 5–15 minutes.

  Serve sprinkled with toasted flaked almonds; you can also top the dessert with low-fat thick (Greek-style) yogurt, thick (heavy/double) cream or fromage frais. (A leftover dessert can be refrigerated and enjoyed the next day.)

Macerated strawberries

Preparation 5 minutes

Cooking None

Quick

No-Cook

For 1

125 g (4 oz) strawberries, halved

2 teaspoons icing (confectioners') sugar

2 teaspoons balsamic vinegar

1/8 teaspoon vanilla extract

1/4 cup (60 ml) thick (heavy/ double) cream

For 2

250 g (8 oz) strawberries, halved

1 tablespoon icing (confectioners') sugar

1 tablespoon balsamic vinegar

1/4 teaspoon vanilla extract

1/2 cup (125 ml) thick (heavy/ double) cream

1 Place the strawberries, icing sugar and vinegar in a bowl. Gently mix to combine and coat the strawberries. Refrigerate for 15 minutes.

2 Mix the vanilla through the cream and serve on top of the strawberries.

Each serving provides
1131 kJ, 270 kcal, 3 g protein, 22 g fat (14 g saturated fat), 13 g carbohydrate (13 g sugars), 3 g fibre, 8 mg sodium

Cook's tip

Macerated strawberries can also be served with your favourite cake or tart.

Other ideas

■ Instead of balsamic vinegar, experiment with liqueurs such as Malibu or Cointreau.

■ Use other fresh seasonal berries as well as, or instead of, strawberries.

Rice pudding

Preparation 5 minutes

Cooking 25 minutes

For 1

¼ cup (60 ml) pouring cream

½ cup (125 ml) milk, plus
    2 tablespoons extra

¼ teaspoon vanilla extract

¼ cup (55 g) medium-grain
    white rice

½ mango, diced, to serve

mint leaf, to garnish

For 2

½ cup (125 ml) pouring cream

1 cup (250 ml) milk, plus
    ¼ cup (60 ml) extra

½ teaspoon vanilla extract

½ cup (110 g) medium-grain
    white rice

1 mango, diced, to serve

mint leaves, to garnish

1 Place the cream in a small saucepan. Add ½ cup (125 ml) milk if cooking for one, and 1 cup (250 ml) milk if cooking for two.

2 Add vanilla and bring the milk to a rolling boil over medium heat. Stir in the rice and gently simmer for 25 minutes, stirring regularly.

3 When the rice is getting dry, stir in the remaining milk. To serve, top with diced mango cheeks and garnish with mint leaf.

Serving suggestion

Rice pudding is delicious on its own, but you can also serve it with poached rhubarb, fresh berries or canned fruit.

Another idea

Add some sliced banana to the rice a few minutes before the end of cooking and serve sprinkled with ground cinnamon.

Each serving provides
2275 kJ, 543 kcal, 10 g protein, 32 g fat (21 g saturated fat),
53 g carbohydrate (10 g sugars), <1 g fibre, 88 mg sodium

Banana and strawberry parfait

Preparation 5 minutes

Cooking None

For 1

⅓ cup (60 g) mascarpone

1½ tablespoons coconut cream

2 teaspoons icing (confectioners')
   sugar

1 banana

4 strawberries

1 coconut macaroon biscuit

For 2

⅔ cup (125 g) mascarpone

¼ cup (60 ml) coconut cream

1 tablespoon icing (confectioners')
   sugar

2 bananas

8 strawberries

2 coconut macaroon biscuits

1 Place the mascarpone, coconut cream and icing sugar in a small bowl, then fold together using a spoon.

2 Cut the banana into 1 cm (½ inch) slices. Cut the strawberries into quarters and roughly crumble the macaroon or macaroons.

3 Place half the banana in one or two 400 ml (14 fl oz) glasses. Top with half the strawberries, then half the macaroon, then dollop with half the mascarpone mixture. Add another layer of banana, strawberries and mascarpone, finally topping with the remaining macaroon.

Each serving provides
2092 kJ, 500 kcal, 6 g protein, 37 g fat (28 g saturated fat), 37 g carbohydrate (33 g sugars), 4 g fibre, 97 mg sodium

Leftover magic

■ Buy coconut cream in small tins, for minimum wastage. It can be refrigerated in an airtight container for up to 5 days. Try some drizzled over fresh fruit or muesli, stir it through a rice pudding, or stir it through creamy Asian-style soups or curries.

■ Mascarpone comes in 250 g (8 oz) tubs. Leftover mascarpone can be refrigerated until the use-by date on the carton. Add a simple dollop to other fresh or poached fruit desserts, or use it as a gourmet spread on sandwiches, wraps and quesadillas. Try it instead of cream or butter, mixed through hot pasta dishes, stirred through soups just before serving, or when making mashed potato.

Other ideas

- Replace the banana with mango or pineapple or peaches, or add an extra fruit variety for a more fruity dessert.

- Instead of the coconut macaroon, use another coconut-based biscuit (cookie) or lightly toasted coconut.

- Drizzle with fresh passionfruit pulp.

- Instead of mascarpone, use whipped cream: beat some whipping cream in a small bowl with electric beaters until soft peaks form, add the coconut cream and 1 teaspoon brown sugar per person, then beat for a further minute or two until the cream thickens again.

Caramelised banana

Preparation 5 minutes

Cooking 5 minutes

For 1

- 1 tablespoon butter
- 1 tablespoon firmly packed brown sugar
- ¼ teaspoon finely grated orange zest
- 1 tablespoon orange juice (optional)
- 1 banana

For 2

- 2 tablespoons butter
- 2 tablespoons firmly packed brown sugar
- ½ teaspoon finely grated orange zest
- 2 tablespoons orange juice (optional)
- 2 bananas

Each serving provides
1150 kJ, 275 kcal, 2 g protein, 16 g fat (10 g saturated fat),
33 g carbohydrate (30 g sugars), 2 g fibre, 141 mg sodium

1 Melt the butter in a small saucepan over low heat. Add the sugar, orange zest, and orange juice if using, and stir until the sugar has dissolved. Simmer for 1 minute.

2 Meanwhile, peel the banana and thickly slice on the diagonal. Add to the pan and stir gently to coat with the caramel. Allow to heat through for 1 minute, then serve.

Serving suggestions

These sticky bananas are delicious with warm pancakes, with a scoop ice cream or dollop of whipped cream.

Other ideas

- Instead of banana, try sliced fresh peaches, or slices of peeled and cored fresh pineapple.
- For a special dessert, try caramelised fresh figs. For each person, cut 1 fresh fig in half lengthwise. Sprinkle with 2 teaspoons brown sugar, dot with 1 teaspoon butter and grill (broil) under medium–high heat for 2 minutes, until the sugar is bubbling. Serve warm, topped with a mixture of 1 tablespoon mascarpone, a few drops of vanilla extract, and ½ teaspoon amaretto or other almond-flavoured liqueur.

Poached pears

Preparation 5 minutes

Cooking 25 minutes

Step-by-step

For 1

1 cup (250 ml) grapefruit juice
½ cup (110 g) sugar
½ vanilla bean
1 firm pear

For 2

1 cup (250 ml) grapefruit juice
½ cup (110 g) sugar
½ vanilla bean
2 firm pears

Each slice provides
1478 kJ, 352 kcal, 1 g protein, <1 g fat
(0 g saturated fat), 88 g carbohydrate
(81 g sugars), 3 g fibre, 10 mg sodium

Step 1   Place the grapefruit juice, sugar and 1 cup (250 ml) water in a small saucepan. Cut the vanilla bean in half lengthwise using a small sharp knife. Scrape the seeds from the vanilla bean into the saucepan, adding the pod as well. Bring to a boil over high heat and cook for a few minutes, until the liquid has reduced to a syrup.

Step 2   Meanwhile, peel the pear or pears and cut in half lengthwise. Remove the round core using a spoon. Place the pear halves in the syrup and cover with a piece of baking (parchment) paper to help submerge them. Simmer for 15 minutes, or until tender.

These pears are superb with cream, yogurt or lemon sorbet. The cooled syrup can be strained and frozen, then used again for poaching.

Step 3
Strain the pears from the syrup, leaving ¼ cup (60 ml) of syrup in the pan. Boil the syrup for 5 minutes to thicken it. Serve the pear halves with the extra syrup drizzled over.

Baked brioche with peaches

Preparation 5 minutes

Cooking 5 minutes

Quick

One-pot

For 1

- 1 individual brioche
- 2 teaspoons raspberry jam
- 1 peach, stoned and cut into wedges or 6 canned peach slices, well drained
- 1 tablespoon mascarpone
- 2 teaspoons toasted flaked almonds

For 2

- 2 individual brioche
- 1 tablespoon raspberry jam
- 2 peaches, stoned and cut into wedges or 12 canned peach slices, well drained
- 2 tablespoons mascarpone
- 1 tablespoon toasted flaked almonds

1 Preheat the oven to 180°C (350°F/Gas 4).

2 Cut the 'ball' off the top of each brioche and cut it in half; set aside. Cut the remaining piece of brioche in half horizontally, through the centre. Spread the cut sides with the jam and place on a baking tray, jam side up.

3 Arrange the peach wedges or slices over the brioche (if desired, arrange in a fan-like pattern). Bake for 5 minutes.

4 Dollop the brioche halves with the mascarpone. Sprinkle with the almonds, top with the reserved brioche pieces and serve.

Each serving provides
2780 kJ, 664 kcal, 11 g protein, 23 g fat (12 g saturated fat), 102 g carbohydrate (74 g sugars), 10 g fibre, 373 mg sodium

Cook's tip

Brioche is a yeasted French bread. Rich and golden and slightly sweet, it makes a simple yet elegant dessert.

Leftover magic

Leftover canned peaches can be refrigerated in their juice in an airtight container for up to 1 week. Use in desserts and fruit salads.

Other ideas

- Spread your favourite jam or marmalade on the brioche.
- Use a croissant instead of the brioche.

Mini bread and butter pudding

For 2

Preparation 5 minutes + 20 minutes standing
- -
Cooking 35 minutes

2 teaspoons butter

2 thick slices raisin toast

1 peach, cut into thin wedges

²/₃ cup (150 ml) milk

²/₃ cup (150 ml) pouring cream

2 tablespoons caster (superfine) sugar

½ teaspoon vanilla extract

2 eggs, lightly beaten

icing (confectioners') sugar, for sprinkling

- -

Each serving provides
2655 kJ, 634 kcal, 13 g protein, 44 g fat
(26 g saturated fat), 47 g carbohydrate
(36 g sugars), 2 g fibre, 229 mg sodium

1 Preheat the oven to 180°C (350°F/Gas 4).

2 Butter the raisin toast on one side, then cut into 1–2 cm (½–¾ inch) cubes. Place the bread cubes and half the peach wedges in a 3½ cup (875 ml) baking dish.

3 Whisk the milk, cream, sugar, vanilla and eggs together in a jug. Pour the mixture over the bread and arrange the remaining peach slices over the top. Leave to stand for 20 minutes, for the bread to absorb the milk.

4 Bake for 30–35 minutes, or until the top is golden and a skewer inserted in the centre comes out clean.

5 Leave at room temperature for 10 minutes. Serve dusted with icing sugar.

Leftover magic

This is a recipe worth making for two. If cooking for one, you can cover the leftover pudding with plastic wrap and refrigerate it for up to 2 days. Simply remove the plastic wrap and reheat in a low oven before serving. Serve with leftover cream.

Instead of raisin toast, use any kind of bread you have on hand or a croissant or panettone.

Cherry and almond sundae

Preparation 5 minutes

Cooking None

Quick

No-Cook

For 1

3 scoops strawberry frozen
yogurt

12 fresh cherries, cut in half,
stones removed

1/4 cup (60 ml) ready-made
chocolate sauce

2 tablespoons roughly chopped
Viennese almonds

For 2

6 scoops strawberry frozen
yogurt

24 cherries, cut in half, stones
removed

1/2 cup (125 ml) ready-made
chocolate sauce

1/3 cup (50 g) roughly chopped
Viennese almonds

1 For each sundae, place 3 scoops of frozen
yogurt in a banana split boat or dessert dish.
Add the cherries and the chocolate sauce and
top with chopped almonds.

2 Serve immediately, before the yogurt melts.

Each serving provides
2163 kJ, 517 kcal, 11 g protein, 17 g fat (7 g saturated fat),
82 g carbohydrate (77 g sugars), 3 g fibre, 131 mg sodium

Other ideas

▪ For a parfait-style sundae, place half the
cherries in the bottom of one or two tall
clear glasses. To each add two scoops of
frozen yogurt, half the chocolate sauce and
1 tablespoon of chopped almonds. Add the
remaining cherries and top with one scoop of
frozen yogurt, then the remaining chocolate
sauce and almonds.

▪ Toasted almonds can be used instead of
Viennese almonds.

▪ Instead of chocolate sauce, try a fruit sauce
or topping.

▪ Make a banana sundae, using sliced bananas,
frozen yogurt and caramel sauce; top with
chopped walnuts.

Trifle

Preparation 5 minutes

Cooking None

For 1

125 g (4 oz) strawberries

1 jam rollette (mini jelly roll)

1 tablespoon orange juice or
sweet sherry

¼ cup (60 ml) ready-made
custard

2 tablespoons thick (heavy/
double) cream

For 2

250 g (8 oz) strawberries

2 jam rollettes (mini jelly rolls)

2 tablespoons orange juice or
sweet sherry

½ cup (125 ml) ready-made
custard

⅓ cup (80 ml) thick (heavy/
double) cream

1 Hull the strawberries and cut into quarters.
Cut the jam rollette or rollettes into slices about
1 cm (½ inch) thick.

2 Arrange half the rollette slices in the base
of one or two small clear glass serving dishes.
Sprinkle with half the orange juice. Arrange
half the strawberries over the top, then pour half
the custard over, spreading it out using the back
of a spoon.

3 Repeat with the remaining rollette slices,
orange juice, strawberries (reserve a few for
the top) and custard to make another layer.

4 Drizzle the cream over, top with reserved
strawberries and serve.

Each serving provides
1652 kJ, 394 kcal, 7 g protein, 26 g fat (15 g saturated fat),
35 g carbohydrate (28 g sugars), 3 g fibre, 196 mg sodium

Leftover magic

- Trifle is the perfect use for any leftover cake that
is going stale. Use it instead of the jam rollettes.

- Use any leftover rollettes, custard and cream for
another quick dessert with your choice of fruit.

Other ideas

- Add your favourite jelly. Cut it into cubes
and layer it with the rollette slices.

- Use savoiardi (lady fingers) instead of the
jam rollettes.

- Instead of strawberries, use other fresh
berries, or a small tub of canned fruit, such
as peaches, pears, apricots or mixed fruit.

Cook's tip

If time allows, refrigerate the trifle for up to
6 hours for the flavours to develop.

For a special celebration, this pretty dessert is a winner. It's worth making for two people, as a leftover jelly can be refrigerated and savoured the next day.

Rose petal jelly

For 2

Preparation 20 minutes + 8 hours refrigeration

- -

Cooking 5 minutes

1 If using gelatine sheets, soak them in cold water for 2–3 minutes to soften them. If using powdered gelatine, sprinkle them into a small cup containing about 2 tablespoons of water and set aside.

2 Put the sugar and ½ cup (125 ml) of the wine in a large saucepan. Stir over medium heat until the sugar has dissolved.

3 Add the gelatine leaves (or the powder and water) to the sugar mixture. Stir until well dissolved, then remove from the heat and leave to cool. Stir in the remaining wine, along with the rosewater and rose petals.

4 Pour the mixture into individual glasses or lightly oiled moulds. Refrigerate for at least 8 hours, or until set.

5 Serve topped with raspberries and cream, if desired.

Cook's tips

▥ Instead of rose petals, you can use borage or scented geranium petals.

▥ There are many varieties of scented geranium, ranging in aroma from apple to nutmeg and mint to pine. Rose- and lemon-scented plants are the best for use in cooking.

4 gelatine sheets, or 2 heaped teaspoons powdered gelatine

⅔ cup (145 g) caster (superfine) sugar

2 cups (500 ml) sparkling wine

1 tablespoon rosewater

18 small rose petals, carefully washed

raspberries and cream, to serve (optional)

- -

Each serving provides
2046 kJ, 488 kcal, 3 g protein, <1 g fat
(<1 g saturated fat), 80 g carbohydrate
(80 g sugars), <1 g fibre, 36 mg sodium

Sweet and savoury sauces

Whether savoury or sweet, a sauce can transform the most simple dish into something special. Having homemade sauce in the freezer, portioned for easy access, makes meal-time a breeze.

Raspberry coulis

Makes about 1 cup (250 ml)

Combine 250 g (8 oz) **raspberries**, 2 tablespoons **icing (confectioners') sugar** and 2 teaspoons **lemon juice** in a food processor and blend until smooth. Pour into a sieve over a bowl, then use the back of a spoon to press out as much liquid as possible, leaving behind the small seeds. Serve with ice cream or cake, pancakes (see pages 214 and 217), French toast (page 218) or ready-made waffles.

Chocolate sauce

Makes about 1 cup (250 ml)

Heat ½ cup (125 ml) **pouring (light) cream** in a small saucepan over low heat. Add 200 g (7 oz) chopped **dark chocolate**, 1 tablespoon **brown sugar** and 1 teaspoon **vanilla extract**. When the chocolate has begun to soften, remove from the heat and stir until smooth.

Vanilla custard for 2

Makes about ⅔ cup (150 ml)

Whisk 1 **egg yolk**, 1 tablespoon **caster (superfine) sugar** and 1 teaspoon **cornflour** (cornstarch) in a small bowl until pale and creamy. Heat ⅔ cup (150 ml) **milk** in a small saucepan just to boiling point. Gradually pour the milk into the egg mixture, stirring constantly.

Wash out the saucepan, then pour in the custard mixture. Using a wooden spoon, stir over low heat, without boiling, for a few minutes, until the custard has thickened and coats the back of the spoon. Stir in ½ teaspoon **vanilla extract** and serve warm or cold. Custard doesn't freeze well, but can be refrigerated in an airtight container for up to 3 days.

Caramel sauce

Makes about 1¼ cups (310 ml)

Place 1 cup (185 g) **brown sugar**, ½ cup (125 ml) **pouring (light) cream**, 100 g (3½ oz) chopped **butter** and 1 teaspoon **vanilla extract** in a small saucepan. Stir over low heat until the mixture has melted and the sauce is smooth.

Apple sauce

Makes about 1 cup (250 ml)

Peel, core and chop 3 granny smith **apples**. Place in a small saucepan with 1 tablespoon **lemon juice** and 1 tablespoon **water**. Bring to a boil, cover and cook over medium heat for 10 minutes, or until the apples are very soft. Stir in 1 tablespoon **sugar**. Leave the sauce chunky, or purée using a hand-held stick blender until smooth. Serve with pork, duck or ham; or add a little more sugar and a tiny pinch of ground cinnamon and serve as a sweet sauce.

Chunky tomato sauce

Makes about 1½ cups (375 ml)

Heat 1 tablespoon **olive oil** in a medium saucepan over medium heat. Add 1 finely chopped small **onion** and cook for 5 minutes, until soft. Add 2 crushed **garlic** cloves and cook for 1 minute more. Stir in a 410 g (15 oz) can chopped **tomatoes**, a pinch of **dried Italian herbs** and 1 tablespoon **tomato paste (concentrated purée)**. Bring to a boil, reduce the heat and simmer for 5 minutes. Season with salt, freshly ground black pepper and a pinch of sugar.

Freezing sauces

Cool your sauce, spoon into ice cube trays and freeze. Once frozen, empty the frozen sauce cubes into a zip-lock bag, expel the excess air and freeze for up to 3 months. To use, take out as many cubes as you need (each one holds about 1 tablespoon of sauce), then reheat gently from frozen — in a small bowl in the microwave is best for small quantities.

Leftover ready-made tomato-based pasta sauces can also be frozen in this way, or in small, airtight, freezer-proof containers.

Serving sizes For most sauces, allow 2–3 tablespoons per serve. For pasta sauce, allow about ½ cup (125 ml) per serve.

Basic white sauce

Makes about 1 cup (250 ml)

Melt 1½ tablespoons **butter** in a small saucepan over medium–low heat. Sprinkle 1 tablespoon **plain (all-purpose) flour** over and cook, stirring, for 1 minute, to cook out the raw flour taste. Add 1 cup (250 ml) **milk** a little at a time, stirring between each addition until smooth. Keep stirring until the mixture boils and thickens, then boil for 1 minute. Season to taste. For cheese sauce, add ¼ cup (30 g) grated cheddar, and a pinch of mustard powder if desired.

Satay sauce

Makes about ½ cup (125 g)

Heat 1 tablespoon **vegetable oil** in a small saucepan over medium heat. Add 2 tablespoons chopped **onion** and cook, stirring, for 2 minutes, or until softened. Stir in 2 tablespoons **crunchy peanut butter**, ⅓ cup (80 ml) **coconut milk** and 2 teaspoons **kecap manis**. Cook, stirring, for 2–3 minutes, or until thickened.

Basil pesto

Makes about ¾ cup (185 g)

Cook ¼ cup (40 g) **pine nuts** in a dry frying pan over medium heat until lightly toasted, stirring often. Transfer to a plate to cool. Wash and dry the leaves from a large bunch of **basil** — about 1¼ cups (65 g); it doesn't have to be exact — and place in a food processor. Add the **pine nuts**, 2 chopped **garlic** cloves and 2 tablespoons finely grated **parmesan** and process until finely chopped. With the motor running, add ⅓ cup (80 ml) extra virgin **olive oil** in a thin stream and process until smooth. Scrape down the sides of the bowl with a spatula and process again briefly. Serve at room temperature, mixed through hot pasta, as a condiment with meat or chicken, or on sandwiches, bruschetta (page 52) or pizza (page 58).

Salad dressings

Use salad dressings sparingly. It's a good idea to keep the dressing separate and simply dress the salad on your plate. This way you can keep any leftover salad for another meal, without it going soggy.

Tangy balsamic dressing

Combine 1 tablespoon **lemon juice**, 2 teaspoons **balsamic vinegar**, 2 teaspoons **vegetable oil**, 1 teaspoon **soy sauce** and a pinch of **sugar** in a small screw-top jar. Seal tightly and shake until evenly combined. Lovely with green salads, or drizzled over grilled (broiled) chicken or salmon.

Tahini dressing

Combine 2 tablespoons **tahini** (sesame paste), 2 tablespoons **natural (plain) yogurt**, about 2 tablespoons **lemon juice** and 1 small crushed **garlic** clove in a small screw-top jar. Seal tightly and shake until evenly combined. Goes well with roast vegetable salads.

Simple creamy dressing

In a small bowl, combine 3 tablespoons **sour cream**, 1 teaspoon chopped fresh or dried **chives**, 1 tablespoon **lemon juice** and ¼ teaspoon **dijon mustard**. Add 1 tablespoon **water** and whisk until evenly combined. This dressing is great with boiled small new potatoes, as well as over salad.

Asian-style dressing

In a screw-top jar, combine 2 tablespoons **lime juice**, 1½ tablespoons **fish sauce**, 1½ tablespoons **brown sugar** and ½ teaspoon chopped **fresh red chilli**. Shake until evenly combined. This dressing is good with cabbage or noodle-based salads as well as drizzled over barbecued fish or chicken.

Warm bacon dressing

Cut 1 slice rindless **bacon** (bacon strip) into short thin strips, then cook in a frying pan in 1 table poon **olive oil** until crisp. Add 2 teaspoons **red wine vinegar** to the pan and swirl to combine. Serve warm over potatoes, or a spinach or mixed leaf salad.

Vinaigrette

Makes just over ⅓ cup (80 ml)

Place ¼ cup (60 ml) **olive oil**, ½ teaspoon **dijon or wholegrain mustard**, and about 1½ tablespoons **vinegar or lemon juice** in a small screw-top jar. Seal tightly and shake until well combined. If you don't have a spare screw-top jar, just whisk the vinaigrette with a fork in small bowl. It keeps in the fridge for up to 1 week.

Variations

- ▪ Use different flavoured vinegars, such as red or white wine vinegar, raspberry or balsamic vinegar, or even a herb-infused vinegar.
- ▪ Try orange or lime juice instead of lemon juice.
- ▪ Use different types of oil, such as walnut, extra virgin olive oil, or light olive oil mixed with a few drops of sesame oil.
- ▪ Add chopped fresh herbs such as chervil, thyme, rosemary, chives or basil.
- ▪ Gently bruise a garlic clove, add it to the dressing and leave to stand for 30 minutes before using, to allow the flavour to permeate. This will add a mild garlic flavour that isn't too overpowering.

Magic mayonnaise

Makes about ½ cup (125 g)

Making mayonnaise isn't as tricky as it sounds. If it saves you a trip to the shop, it's well worth it. It will keep in the fridge in an airtight container for up to 1 week.

Place 1 **egg yolk**, ½ teaspoon **dijon mustard** and 1 teaspoon **lemon juice** in a small bowl. Beat until well combined, using electric beaters. Add ½ cup (125 ml) **vegetable oil or light olive oil**, a few drops at a time at first, beating constantly. As the mixture begins to thicken, you can add the oil in a slow, thin stream. Stir in an extra 1 teaspoon lemon juice and season with salt and ground **white pepper**.

Variations

- ▪ **For aïoli,** replace the mustard with 1 small crushed garlic clove.
- ▪ **For tartare sauce,** add 1 finely chopped spring onion (scallion), 2 teaspoons chopped capers, 2 teaspoons chopped gherkins (pickles) and 2 teaspoons finely chopped fresh parsley.
- ▪ **For seafood cocktail sauce,** add 2 tablespoons tomato sauce (ketchup), 2 tablespoons pouring (light) cream, 1 teaspoon worcestershire sauce and a few drops of Tabasco sauce.
- ▪ **For ranch dressing,** add ¼ cup (60 ml) buttermilk, ¼ teaspoon dried chives, a pinch of garlic powder and a pinch of onion powder. Season with salt and freshly ground black pepper.

Index

Index of quick recipes

When you want some lovely food in a flash, here's a handy index of all the 'Quick' recipes in this book, which you can dish up in 30 minutes or under. To make it even easier, we've divided the recipes even further into different categories, so you can see at a glance which recipes match your time and energy levels.

On the table in 15 minutes

On the table in 20 minutes

On the table in 25 minutes

On the table in 30 minutes

NO-COOK recipes

Note to readers

Weights and measures

Australian cup and spoon measurements have been used throughout this book: 1 cup = 250 ml; 1 tablespoon = 20 ml; 1 teaspoon = 5 ml. If using smaller cup and spoon measures (where 1 cup = 235 ml and 1 tablespoon = 15 ml), adjust the recipe accordingly. A small variation in the weight or volume of most ingredients is unlikely to adversely affect a recipe.

Cup and spoon measures are level, unless stated otherwise. Ingredients are generally listed by their weight or volume with cup measurements given for convenience, unless the conversion is imperfect, whereby the ingredients are listed by weight or volume only.

Sometimes conversions within a recipe are not exact but are the closest conversion that is a suitable measurement for each system. Use either the metric or the imperial measurements; do not mix the two systems.

Oven temperatures

These recipes have been written for a regular oven. If you have a fan-forced (convection) oven, reduce the temperature by 20°C (68°F). If you have a broiler (grill) where the temperature cannot be adjusted by a temperature dial or knob, lower the rack down from the element as follows:
Medium: about half or two-thirds of the way down.
Medium–hot: about a third of the way down.

Can sizes

Can sizes vary between countries and manufacturers; if the stated size is unavailable, use the nearest equivalent. For example: 225 g = 8 oz; 300 g = 10 oz; 350 g = 12 oz; 400/410 g = 14 oz = 398 ml/410 ml; 425 g = 15 oz = 540 ml; 800 g = 28 oz = 796 ml.

Ingredients

If using raw eggs in a recipe, make sure the shells are not cracked or dirty. Keep eggs refrigerated at 5°C (40°F) or below, use them within five weeks of purchase and observe the 'use by' date. If you are concerned about the risk of Salmonella, do not serve foods made with raw eggs to pregnant women, young children, elderly people or anyone with an illness or damaged immune system.

Where stock is mentioned, it is assumed to be salt-reduced. Using salted commercial stock will give a higher sodium content than indicated in the recipe's nutritional analysis.

Nutritional Analysis

Each recipe is accompanied by a nutrient profile showing kilojoules (kJ), calories (kcal), protein, fat (including saturated fat), carbohydrate (including sugars), fibre and sodium. <1 means it is less than 1 g. Serving suggestions, garnishes and optional ingredients are not included.

Alternative terms and substitutes

capsicum bell pepper, sweet pepper

corn cob mealie/miele

cos lettuce romaine lettuce

cream where type of cream is not specified, use pure, light, single, or pouring cream

eggplant aubergine, brinjal

English spinach baby spinach; not the heavily veined, thick-leafed vegetable sold as spinach or silver beet

filo phyllo

fresh shiitake mushrooms rehydrated dried shiitake mushrooms

hokkien noodles 2-minute noodles or other fast-cooking noodle

kecap manis sweet soy sauce

Lebanese cucumber Mediterranean cucumber, short cucumber

ling use any firm-white-fleshed fish such as cod, coley, hake or kabeljou

low-fat milk 1% milk

oregano oreganum

papaya pawpaw

passionfruit granadilla

rice noodles rice vermicelli

salt-reduced low-sodium

self-raising flour self-rising flour

silverbeet Swiss chard, often sold as spinach in South Africa

Swiss brown mushrooms brown mushrooms

vanilla extract vanilla essence

vegetable oil use canola oil

wholegrain mustard seeded mustard

zucchini baby marrow, courgette

Cooking for One or Two

Recipes Jo Forrest, Tracy Rutherford, Kerrie Sun,
    Gabrielle Wheatley

Editor Katri Hilden

Designer Susanne Geppert

Senior Designer Donna Heldon

Photographer Steve Brown; (Ian Hoffstetter p. 41)

Stylist Trish Heagerty; (Janelle Bloom p. 121, p. 173, p. 229)

Home Economist Nick Eade; (Wendy Quisumbing
    p. 41, p. 121, p. 173, p. 229)

Nutritional Analysis Toni Gumley

Proofreader Susan McCreery

Indexer Diane Harriman

Production Controller Anne Schwertfeger

Editorial Project Manager General Books Deborah Nixon

Reader's Digest General Books

Editorial Director Lynn Lewis

Managing Editor Rosemary McDonald

Art Director Carole Orbell

Cooking for One or Two is published by
Reader's Digest (Australia) Pty Limited,
80 Bay Street, Ultimo NSW 2007, Australia
www.readersdigest.com.au, www.readersdigest.co.nz,
www.readersdigest.co.za, www.rdasia.com, www.rd.com,
www.readersdigest.ca, www.readersdigest.co.uk

This edition first published 2012

National Library of Australia Cataloguing-in-Publication entry
    Title: Cooking for one or two: more than 100 recipes
    just for you, or maybe two.
    ISBN: 978-1-921744-64-8 (hbk.)
    ISBN: 978-1-921744-65-5 (pbk.)
    Notes: Includes index.
    Subjects: Cooking for one. Cooking for two.
    Dewey Number: 641.561

With thanks to Mud Australia for props for photography.

Prepress by Sinnott Bros, Sydney
Printed and bound by Leo Paper Products, China

We are interested in receiving your comments on
the contents of this book. Write to:
The Editor, General Books Editorial,
Reader's Digest (Australia) Pty Limited,
GPO Box 4353, Sydney, NSW 2001,
or email us at bookeditors.au@readersdigest.com

To order additional copies of this book, please contact
us as follows:
www.readersdigest.com.au, 1300 300 030 (Australia);
www.readersdigest.co.nz, 0800 400 060 (New Zealand);
www.readersdigest.co.za, 0800 980 572 (South Africa);
www.rdasia.com; www.rd.com; www.readersdigest.ca;
www.readersdigest.co.uk
or email us at customerservice@readersdigest.com.au

Concept code: US 0014HM/IC
Product codes: 041 4717 (hbk), 041 4718 (pbk)
041 1330 (hbk, North America)

Mini bread and butter pudding Eggs florentine

chicken noodle soup TUNA STEAK WITH SALSA ROSSA

...as with... lamb cutlets Spiced fruit and nut bread

...ACHED PEARS STEP-BY-STEP Ricotta pancakes with fresh

...usted quail with couscous CARAMELISED BANANA

...ck ideas for... one-pot pasta meals Refrigerator biscuits

...erry whip LEMON AND SAFFRON RISOTTO STEP-BY-STE...

Couscous and chickpea salad Macaroni bake

...ortuguese prawns Step-by-step Macerated strawberries,

...ea chicken fillets Hearty potato soup Brown fried ric...

Prosciutto, pear and parmesan salad Pasta primavera

...NY MEALS FROM ONE BOLOGNESE SAUCE Duck salad

...ck ideas for... stewed fruit Fresh tuna and green bean sa...

...EAN TORTILLA BASKET Prosciutto stuffed chicken

Spiced spatchcock Step-by-step

…RN SOUP INTO A MEAL   Quick ideas for... side salads
…ermilk pancakes   Step-by-step   SPEEDY BOUILLABAISSE   Ba…
…an-fried pork chops   Baked fish parcel   Veal escalope…
Quick ideas for... pizza   Trifle   Cherry and alm…
Grilled mushrooms on ciabatta
CHEF'S SALAD   Quick and healthy m…
Asian rice salad   ROAST BEEF DINNER   Mini lamb roa…
…cchini SCRAMBLED EGGS WITH SMOKED SALMON STEP-BY…
…tewed fruit Roast chicken Maryland   Miso soup with to…
…mustard salmon   Fruit smoothie   Linguine with salmo…
Lamb and ginger stir-fry Pork patty with tomato and…
…pilaf   Many meals from one Beef stew   Cheese souff…
Chicken fajitas   Fresh rice paper rolls   THAI BEEF RED…
…UICK IDEAS FOR... SALAD LEAVES   Baked egg pots RIS…